Praise for *The Path Redefined*

"Lauren's book is not only full of great advice to aspiring entrepreneurs, but also has a lot of inspirational thoughts and tips for those of us already in the midst of our entrepreneurial careers. I'm glad she took the time to share her energy and her wisdom."

JOE LONSDALE,
General Partner of Venture Capital Firm 8VC

"*The Path Redefined* is an honest and candid overview of how Lauren has forged her brand and what it takes for a forward-looking individual to build success on their own terms. This book will inspire anyone from a college graduate just building out their career to a seasoned executive seeking a passion pivot. One of the most important lessons I gleaned from the book was about the power of personal brand and reputation and the control we have over others' perceptions of us. 'Interactions you have with a client, colleague, or friend today may be the unofficial interview for your dream job in three years.' It's important for entrepreneurs to build for their future every day, and with this book, Lauren has done just that. Brava!"

MORIN OLUWOLE,
Luxury and Digital Strategy Advisor

"*The Path Redefined* is a great read for the entrepreneur in all of us. It offers insights as applicable for the twenty-something as for the individual getting ready to launch that encore career. Looking forward to seeing what Lauren accomplishes in her next twenty-eight years and beyond."

MATTHEW HARRINGTON,
Global President and Chief Operating Officer of Edelman PR

"Lauren epitomizes her generation—they are the most knowledgeable, responsible, and powerful generation of young adults the world has ever seen. They understand better than anyone how to leverage digital and social media to drive and effect positive change in the world, and they are creating new business models where purpose drives profit. Not only can we learn a huge amount from Lauren and her insightful book *The Path Redefined*, but I have a feeling she and her peers will succeed, where we failed, in driving the world to a better place."

DAVID JONES,
Founder and CEO of The Brandtech Group

"*The Path Redefined* is a must-read for those looking to succeed on their own terms. Lauren, a true go-getter and successful entrepreneur, shares her own life experiences and valuable advice that are sure to motivate and inspire readers to go after their goals!"

ERIC RIPERT,
Chef and Co-Owner of Le Bernardin

"Daily, you walk around with two of the most priceless assets out there—your brain and your attitude. *The Path Redefined* will show you how to make the most of both. With her trademark wit and verve, Lauren teaches you how to prepare, take charge, course correct, and shine. Importantly, Lauren's advice isn't theoretical—she's already demonstrated its enormous power with her own entrepreneurial success. If you are looking to journey the entrepreneurial road less traveled, let *The Path Redefined* be your definitive guide."

MANISHA THAKOR,
Trustee, Independent Mutual Fund Board of Directors
and Lincoln Variable Insurance Products Trust

"Lauren has achieved great success early in life because she capitalized on her unique personal talents. She creates solutions to problems and simplifies the complex. In *The Path Redefined*, Lauren inspires others to actualize their full potential in each area of their lives and shares many of the lessons that allow her to keep going."

MARCUS SAMUELSSON,
Chef, Restaurateur, Author, Activist

"The book is an inspirational ride—a ride that makes the reader feel fearless! Lauren reminds us that nothing is beyond our reach and somehow gives us all longer arms just so we can reach a tiny bit more. Like the author herself, the book is beautiful inside and out."

GAIL BECKER,
Founder and CEO of Caulipower

"Lauren is one of the smartest, most ambitious, resourceful, and tenacious people I've ever met. Her business acumen and insights into how to leverage her uniqueness are both relevant and refreshing. *The Path Redefined* is a must-read for anyone interested in knowing the keys to achieving modern-day success. It will be an indispensable tool to men who want to understand the businesswomen of the twenty-first century."

ROBERT G. CLARK,
Executive Chairman and Founder of CLAYCO

THE
PATH
REDEFINED

Getting to the Top on Your Own Terms

LAUREN MAILLIAN

Story **BUILDERS** P R E S S

Published by StoryBuilders Press
eBook: 978-1-954521-78-0
Paperback: 978-1-954521-79-7
Hardcover: 978-1-954521-80-3

Contents

Introduction

Life dealt me a blow ... And I needed a new plan.

Every day felt like a battle, losing ground bit by bit—strength, momentum, and pride were slipping away.

I had to reclaim my ambitions, my family, and my sense of self ... I had to stop the slow erosion that threatened to consume me ... To stop feeling I was merely surviving through the heaped responsibilities weighed on my shoulders.

And despite trying all the conventional wisdom—about being a successful entrepreneur and a present parent—I often felt incomplete and overwhelmed.

In moments like this, so many of the philosophies I had earlier on and wrote within the pages of *The Path Redefined* became the advice I took to change my own life.

Throughout the years, I have gathered so many new lessons through life circumstances and unexpected opportunities worth sharing.

MY NAME IS LAUREN MAILLIAN

I don't often dwell on past struggles, but you may know parts of my journey.

Years ago, I stood at a crossroads as a single mother, emerging from a turbulent divorce that shattered my world. The fallout stripped away stability, leaving me to accept what I considered a painful defeat at the time and forge ahead alone, fighting to build a future for my children and myself.

I battled a health crisis that completely changed my life view, one that left me scared to my bones about what would become of my family, my aspirations, and the life I wanted to build.

I've hosted a prime-time television show on NBC's Oxygen Network, alongside Randi Zuckerberg, Ido Leffler, and Sarah Prevette, called *Quit Your Day Job*, which launched me into the world of media as an expert, commentator, and a trusted voice but what you don't know is that opportunity came with its share of disappointment as I saw that dream come to an abrupt and disappointing end.

These experiences are only a scratch on the surface but every one of them molded me into the resilient entrepreneur and advisor I am today.

As a marketer and strategist, I continued to work with iconic brands. Finally, I achieved my dream of joining boards: from advisory boards to boards of directors and overall next-level board opportunities like joining the advisory board of a publicly traded health tech company.

I also did something I never thought I would do, which was con-templating going into corporate America and taking my talents to the Fortune 1 Walmart after getting to know the company in 2019 and being appointed to the first-ever Board of Disruption by Marc Lore, the former President and CEO of Walmart U.S. eCommerce and founder of Jet.com. But that didn't happen in the way I envisioned it. Something smaller came my way, which gave me the platform that would eventually catapult my thought leadership.

These experiences make me think back to every chapter in the book that truly is the most relevant and applicable advice for who I was and where I wanted to go. So many times, I came back to my own book as my compass when I felt uneasy about exactly what to do next or how to make it happen. Today, I pinch myself looking at how much I've accomplished and how quickly I've been able to close gaps.

Like gaps of income from when I first wrote this book as an entirely single mom struggling to find my way to stay afloat in New York City with skyrocketing private school tuition and camp expenses and trying to provide the best opportunities for my two little children all on my own with no child support. That reality eventually became me being able to not only make up for the child support I should have received and never got but also to create something far bigger and better than ever imagined was possible for me to do by myself.

It exceeds what little Lauren thought she could do for herself, for Jayden, and for Chloe. I found myself taking risks again, from professional risks to personal risks of emotion, love, and vulnerability, which made me a better mother, better advisor, a better partner, and better leader.

Time showed me how to really get comfortable with being uncomfortable because my circumstances challenged me to be more vulnerable than I ever thought I would be again. Time also allowed me to grow as a businesswoman in new spaces. I learned to look past imposter syndrome, as I had become known as so many things to so many people—the youngest self-made winery owner in the U.S., the Impact 100 entrepreneur, the single Black mom, the unapologetic girl on a mission.

I was the person that so many didn't understand for a while, and then I think the world caught up to my vision and what I had been trying to build toward as a multi-hyphenate. Or maybe the world changed and so did its examples of success. Or maybe I changed in the world as it was evolving . . . Maybe we are all trying to figure out The Path Redefined to get to the next place, a better place. We all want that, right?

For the first time in my life, I am actually okay with the unknown. I'm okay with not having all of the answers, and I'm also really satisfied with everything that I have right now. If I have more in the future, amazing. But if this is the height of where I am and what I get to do and see and achieve, that is absolutely okay with me too. I've already blown my own mind.

I think the beauty of *The Path Redefined* has always been the ability to do what you love and call it work because then it's never really work at all. That's why the chapter "Build a Life That's Serendipitous by Design" was so powerful for so many readers. When you can find success within the intersections of your expertise, your lived experience, your values, your interests, and your passions, you really do get to live a life that is serendipitous by design. When done well, with great purpose and effort, a life that is serendipitous by design can also be the most successful construct for a life you dreamed of.

So many opportunities have come to me in the past ten years or so. I've watched how I deal with those opportunities in building the next level of *The Path Redefined*. Things that I used to jump up and down for and scream and get thrilled about still hold the same excitement but now get a different response. There's control, there's strategy, there's confidence. There is a certitude with excitement now that I didn't always have before. That certitude has allowed me to level-set which opportunity is right for me and my life, for my family, and for my children. I can assess which opportunity aligns with my goals or which opportunity just excites me the most.

And I think we can all agree that we don't live a life or want to live a life based on excitement alone. That's why purpose really has to be at the center of the biggest decisions that we make and why we make them. But I certainly understand being at the point in life where we don't feel we have the luxury to make all of our decisions led by our purpose. I know because I spent nearly nine years as a single mom making decisions led by my circumstances. And in those moments I felt like I was not in control. Life was happening to me and not for me. No one thought that from the outside looking in. Everyone thought I had a plan.

The experiences gathered over these past ten years or so have opened new doors and gotten me into meetings to consider being a partner with Serena Williams, working with Mare Lore, and some of the greatest founders, business leaders, and brands in the world. I think what we're all hoping for is that one day the people who were on our wish list become the people who one day look at us and say, "Hey, let's collaborate. How can I work with you?"

That has happened to me repeatedly since writing *The Path Redefined*, and I've learned so much along the way that I now really want to uncover and share with you because I've still done it all fairly young, fairly early, and against every single odd and obstacle that was put in my place.

I've done it as a Black woman who lived through the modern-day racial reckoning, a pandemic, and some of the greatest social tensions of our time, while trying to navigate my life, career, and parenthood as the world was turning upside down. All while finding my place, my voice, taking care of my family, achieving my dreams, and creating new structures for success, love, and the future.

I think that really is what *The Path Redefined* is all about. That every mustard seed that we plant, truly can be our greatest harvest in the future. We have to believe it, we have to want it, we have to prepare for it, and we have to strategize for it. That's what I hope I can help you do with this edition of *The Path Redefined*.

Part of my strategy has been expanding my investing work from Angel Investments to helping engineer an $85 million personal care

CPG deal in the growth equity space for a Black female founder with some of the greatest banks in the world.

I've also gone on to be an investor and advisor of the Athena Consumer Acquisition Corporation and announced a $913 million, that's right—nearly $1 billion deal to take e.GO Mobile public. In November 2021, at thirty-six years old, I was taking Athena public, ringing the bell as the youngest Black woman to be part of a Special Purpose Acquisition Company (SPAC), used as a vehicle to take companies public.

I've continuously blown my mind, and I think that one of the most difficult challenges is meeting new people who don't know my story or my struggle and only see success. It makes me so uncomfortable to meet people today who don't know what I've been through.

That's been something difficult to navigate because nobody ever says that *The Path Redefined* means that people will meet you where your story began. It means that they will meet you along your journey and they'll have glimpses into who you are. They'll only have glimpses into all that you had to endure to get to where you are today.

One of the major themes of my journey when I first wrote *The Path Redefined* was navigating through life and my career as a single mother. Since then, I have learned so much, particularly in getting married again. There's a vulnerability in opening up and being willing to be hurt again, being willing to commit again. That personal growth has been a big theme in my life since I wrote the book. The idea of falling in love again is something that all women are becoming more and more open to, whereas I think the old-school mentality was you had your man and that was one and done.

I find this resonates and so many women are getting comfortable finally saying, "This relationship didn't work out right." There is a whole movement. No one can bully you into the "I was going to be with this person for forty, fifty years" mentality. I was open to finding love again and there are ways in which that changed my life, my career, and the risks I've chosen to take.

While writing *The Path Redefined*, I saw myself beginning to pull back from opportunities that were coming to me. Not because I didn't want them, wasn't qualified for them, or didn't have the expertise or the interest. I pulled back because I couldn't imagine raising my kids that way, always being gone, meeting the demands of the most senior and influential roles that were coming my way, and trying to be an involved parent. I felt like the odds were stacked against me to be successful even though the opportunities were being presented to me. It all feels very different when you do have a partner who can help hold down the fort at home.

A key part of *The Path Redefined* is recognizing the impact of my decision to remarry—how it shaped my life, my children's lives, and their confidence. A lot of the things that I wrote about in worry and faced with uncertainty ten years ago are part of what I now do with ease.

There is beauty in telling your story, paying it forward, finding the lessons, and remembering the solutions so that you can share them with others. Here's to *The Path Redefined* helping you achieve your ultimate success on your own terms.

1

This Entrepreneurial Life

THIS ENTREPRENEURIAL LIFE HAS CHANGED
even more than I have transformed. It has dramatically shifted
since I became an entrepreneur twenty years ago and since I wrote
this book ten years ago. But I didn't become an entrepreneur overnight
or even on my own. Every entrepreneur has key people in their life
who provide influence and guidance, help with making connections,
and are there to celebrate successes and mourn failures.

I must tell you, it is easier to find people who celebrate with you
than those who mourn your failures. And I'm not speaking of just
professional failures because our personal experiences significantly
impact professional growth and development. I also speak of my fair
share of personal missed and mourned experiences and opportunities
that have impacted my entrepreneurial life in no small way. Some I
am finally able to share in the pages of this book, experiences that

many thought would end my career but ultimately taught me the true nature of success and launched me into it.

When I started my very first company, having an exit in the tens of millions of dollars was considered a huge success. Now, the landscape has evolved to include billion-dollar valuations and exits for the lucky few. There are now entrepreneurs whose companies get acquired by multi-billion-dollar companies in what is known as an "acquihire" situation.

This is where a company is acquired, and its employees are hired by the acquiring company. For example, Bonobos, a clothing company in the U.S., was sold to Walmart, and the founder, Andy Dunn, who started this cool, edgy menswear company, went on to work at Walmart as an SVP for three years.

What's so interesting is he went on to author a book where he mirrors the broader experiences of many entrepreneurs who grapple with the hidden costs of ambition, and exposes the intense emotional toll of the entrepreneurial journey. Many of my entrepreneurial friends have become employees, with their companies acquired, or have decided they are better off building something that already exists, getting bigger and better at gaining a small piece of equity in something they didn't originally found.

And now, all of a sudden, there are countless ways to be an entrepreneur that didn't even exist when I started my company twenty years ago. We have the gig economy, remote work, coaches, influencers, and media personalities. And if you're like me, if you've already been a thriving entrepreneur for years, you may often find yourself comparing your accomplishments with those of someone who just started on TikTok yesterday. This entrepreneurial life has changed. It has changed for me, it has changed for the world, and it can change for you.

In the past ten years of my life, I've learned what signs are meant to tell us that it's time to truly move on and if it's a blessing in disguise that we should stay a little longer to transform and grow. The funny thing about life is that the signs are always clearer when the storm has passed. And all these years later, I've gone through so many storms and I've always been more than okay. I guess learning to weather storms gracefully really is a secret weapon for success.

When I originally wrote *The Path Redefined*, I was focused on mitigating risk and providing for my children at that point in my life. A lot of those stories and principles are still true; they are incredible. But I hadn't experienced the moments and opportunities that I now have in the past ten years. These have been life-expanding, career-making moments and insanely valuable lessons worth sharing.

Back in 2014, I was this young woman who had a lot of interest and excitement. I had done a lot of work on projects for a lot of companies, but I was not the person who had a lot of the achievements that allow you to play in bigger spaces, make more money, have more influence and more senior connections. I didn't have enough history with people then. Meanwhile, I was in my twenties.

It's not just who you know, it's how you meet them and how long you've known them. For a lot of years in my career, I felt like I wasn't being chosen for the big opportunities. I found it so hard to go from the entrepreneur that felt so successful starting my business at nineteen and exiting at twenty-six, to then leaping from Sugarleaf Vineyards and feeling a sense of imposter syndrome.

I felt I had an identity crisis back then, from ages twenty-six to twenty-seven. Selena Cuffe was my very first client for my business venture, LMB Group which I still run to this day. LMB Group has always been LMB Group, but it was a DBA—doing business as—that stood for Luxury Market Branding. I started LMB Group because it was connected to wine and spirits and hospitality, which I knew well.

Selena was the very first person then to say "You got this. There is so much more to you, Lauren, than just being the youngest self-made winery owner in the country. Yes, it's an award-winning internationally recognized vineyard and winery, but you're going to do so many more things."

I remember asking myself, *Well, what am I going to do?*

Selena and I wrote about this experience in *The Path Redefined* and how she said, "These are all the things. This is all the knowledge you have as a winery owner and the success that you've created in that company and how quickly you've grown that brand to such acclaim. I need all of that for the wines in my portfolio and I need help bringing the Mandela Family wine to the United States." We went on that unforgettable trip to South Africa together and now I have to say *The Path Redefined* has continued to evolve me in the past decade as I lived the advice written on these pages in all the days since it first came out.

Before *The Path Redefined* was published ten years ago, I had an incredible book tour. I traveled across the country, and my book received widespread attention with articles written about it everywhere.

As it was about to be released, I became represented by WME (William Morris Endeavor), one of the world's leading agencies in entertainment, media, and sports. It was Alexis Ohanian, who is now married to Serena Williams, who made the introduction to his team at WME. He said, "Hey, they want to meet you. They want to talk to you," and that moment marked the beginning of a significant new chapter in my career.

For the past ten years, I've worked with WME as my agents, focusing on building and expanding my personal brand. With WME in my corner, a series of TV show opportunities began to emerge, aligning more closely with how I wanted to be seen in the public eye.

One of the most notable opportunities was being a part of the TV show *Quit Your Day Job*. The show, which aired on Oxygen's NBC, was a unique blend of advising, business strategy, and brand-building, focusing on inclusive entrepreneurship and investment. Our greatest competition was *Shark Tank* and *The Apprentice*. Alongside Randi Zuckerberg, Ido Leffler, and Sarah Prevette, I was the only Black woman on prime-time television in a start-up investing role. The show premiered on March 30, 2016, and it was a pivotal moment in my career, propelling me into the media spotlight as a nationally recognized on-air talent and voice.

> Because you see, not every open door is truly meant for you. Some seemingly significant opportunities can lead to the downfall of one's career, business, or life.

Prior to this, I had been offered several TV opportunities. When I had my vineyard and winery, I was even approached to join *The Real Housewives of D.C.* I declined the offer, but a good friend of mine, Stacie, accepted, and they featured my vineyard in one episode of the show.

I had also been offered various other TV roles, including appearances on style shows and as a judge on a modeling competition. However, these opportunities did not align with my vision of being recognized as a serious entrepreneur and businesswoman.

Because you see, not every open door is truly meant for you. Some seemingly significant opportunities can lead to the downfall of one's career, business, or life. And despite my past as a model, I was determined to shape how the world perceived me and to be seen as a business leader.

The opportunity to be on *Quit Your Day Job* was a significant breakthrough, allowing me to present myself in a professional light that reflected my true passions and aspirations.

We're in 2025, eleven years since the book came out and twelve years since I was writing it between 2013 and 2014. Eleven years and so many new experiences. There have been so many changes; with everything that's happened to me, even in the last three years, I have held positions I could only dream of when I first wrote it. I have evolved into a 3x entrepreneur, global investor, advisor, and board director.

Last year, I stepped down after serving as president of a Black-owned media and ad tech company, having met and exceeded a multi-year goal in just months. In the first edition of *The Path Redefined*, I spoke about my introduction to digitalundivided and my love for the mission. There are words from Kathryn Finney, the founder and CEO I took over from, but not because I wanted to take over. I was never expecting to take over.

I joked with everyone that it was my unexpected COVID-19 job and that somehow I'd gone from being the "boss," Chair of the Board of Directors at digitalundivided, to being internally demoted but externally promoted to the role of CEO—where I reported to the board and was no longer a voting member. Now, I'm sitting here having this wild "aha" moment in my life, and I am eleven years from where I was when I called the same people for the same issues, hurdles, and concerns.

Selena is the same person I lean on in times of doubt or difficulty in my career when I find myself questioning what to do next. She's the person I'm calling right now as I'm dealing with everything that I legally can't even talk about—nothing bad professionally, but confidentiality is key when the stakes are high and the contracts are ironclad as they should be. I look back and understand that digitalundivided was a movement and it made me fall in love with its mission from the very first Focus 100 conference—I was the keynote of the conference, judged the pitch competition, and met many founders who have gone on to be leaders in the start-up and venture space.

Over the years as the movement took shape, with many early meetings in my kitchen and living room in Harlem, an organization was born and built by Kathryn Finney. She had the vision for the organization, I had the love for the cause and the audibility in the space as an investor and entrepreneur. I saw value in digitalundivided as a non-profit organization, never thinking that I would even join its board. I didn't know if it would even have a board; it was still a movement. Regardless, I felt compelled by the mission and I was always there. I cherish the memories of the events held in my living room in Harlem, convening incredible women like Stacy Brown-Philpot, who went on to become CEO of TaskRabbit and Asmau Ahmed, who's now a leader within Alphabet for X Development, formerly known as Google X.

When I think about all the people that I met then that I'm still working with today, but at the next level, I would've never imagined that I'd be asked to run and be unanimously voted into the position of CEO at digitalundivided. I would've never imagined leading a non-profit organization in my thirties. I thought that was a cool retirement job. Maybe I'd have done it in my fifties or my sixties for fun or even start my own foundation or organization.

It wasn't the job I was looking for, or that I wanted. It wasn't the big job that I thought I was going to get at Walmart, where I had been serving on the first-ever Board of Disruption.

I was the only Black woman on a board of ten people, seven of whom were global leaders within Walmart and the group of companies, a board member of Walmart and the Walton family, Steuart Walton, myself, and Bharat Anand, Vice Provost for Advances in Learning at Harvard.

That was the most incredible experience in my career at that time. After serving on that board all of 2019 and 2020, helping to drive innovation, I had a series of amazing calls with executive talent recruitment for an incredible role. Just as that formal offer letter arrived, so did COVID-19, and the world came to a stop.

Walmart could no longer hire officer positions, which was the highest level of leadership that I was up for.

Simultaneously, Kathryn Finney decided to make her departure from digitalundivided in the midst of the racial reckoning and the onset of COVID-19. I had been serving as Chair of the Board for an organization that I cared for deeply and its mission. All of a sudden, I'm thirty-five years old, running this small one-million-dollar nonprofit. I knew nothing about writing grants, and I knew nothing about how to lead a nonprofit.

Everything I'd ever done in social impact was because I wanted to, because I thought and felt it was the right thing to do. Not necessarily because I had read the latest and greatest research across the entire sector on solutions, but because I was observant of the ecosystem and I was in tune with what was happening. When I first came into the role, it was me who insisted on adding "Interim" to the title of CEO because I didn't know if I wanted to be there that long, because again, it wasn't that big next-level corporate opportunity.

If I was going to go in-house and go corporate, I was going to Fortune 1. I was going to Walmart and to work with *the* Marc Lore, the "LeBron James of eCommerce," and Janey Whiteside, who had recently come over from American Express as the first-ever Chief Customer Officer. If I went in-house, I was going to work with the greatest of the greats. But that's not how it ended up.

When the board initially asked me to be CEO I said no. I remember thinking I really want to go get my big job, not a small nonprofit. I love the mission, but I want to chair the board. I want to serve in that capacity and be helpful at the highest level. But that's not the plan I guess God had, because there I was being asked to serve as CEO. I insisted on interim at that point, not because I didn't think I could do the work, but because I didn't know how quickly I could achieve my vision to make it something that I was going to want to put my name on.

I knew that if I went to this little nonprofit, I couldn't leave it a little nonprofit. If Lauren Maillian is only known to do big things, I felt that I had to come to digitalundivided and do big things.

I couldn't just come in and maintain the status quo. And I felt that all eyes were on me as a young self-made Black woman who had been making bets in the start-up and tech space. I had been engineering my life and my career to be able to serve on boards that are now finally taking an interest in me. But it's not by happenstance. It's not what people think.

I've always wanted to serve on boards. This is not because it's now become a trend or popular in conversation: women on boards, Black women on boards.

I've wanted to be a Black woman on a board for over a decade, and that's exactly why I served on the boards that I did. I served on the board at the Metropolitan Museum of Art Multicultural Audience Development Advisory Board for ten years because I knew that it would show my ability to serve on an institutional board and a nonprofit board. It taught me great organizational governance at the highest and greatest level.

I knew that I wanted to be on the LIQS board because I wanted to go through building a consumer liquor brand again from the ground up in another sector to validate my ability to do so. After founding Sugarleaf Vineyards, I wanted to prove that I wasn't just the Black woman who could create the first Black-owned winery on the East Coast and become the youngest self-made winery owner in the country. I wanted to prove that Sugarleaf Vineyards' success was not just by coincidence and that I actually built an incredible brand in record time.

I guess it's the same feeling I had when I came to digitalundivided and thought, Okay, I'm here. Everybody knows I'm here now. There's an announcement, if it's on social media, I can't hide from it. I'm not hiding from it if it's an organization I'm proud of. But now, if I'm going to be here, people are going to expect me to do something outsized. They're going to expect me to do something innovative and audacious, not just for the culture but for women, and not just for women, but because I'm Lauren.

It's finally dawning on me that this is the reputation that I have across sectors. And I don't say that in a boastful way, I say that because it's finally dawned on me what people mean when they say that I wasn't really seeing it for myself, because I was in it and never stepped back. I think it's the pressure that I put on myself to help every single Black and Latina woman I've known over the years.

During one of our digitalundivided events, BREAKTHROUGH LA, EnJunaya Canton of Zuhuri Beauty recounted how we met years before. HSN had hired me to do a mentorship program and I happened to mentor her then. Years later, she applied for BREAKTHROUGH. I didn't flag her for selection, I just asked the team to reach out to her to encourage her to apply, as we were creating a list of people to reach out to in case they didn't know about the organization or the opportunity.

I did not judge or review EnJunaya's application. She got in on her own merit and it became one of the many full-circle moments that I had while at digitalundivided. I was able to help founders that I'd met before, founding the same company or building a different one that was sparked from the initial idea.

Something similar happened in Dallas with Janelle Langford's company, which applied for our BREAKTHROUGH cohort there. I'd known her years earlier as a PR pro. Now, she is a founder.

I think about all the women that were already reaching out to me, that I was able to support through digitalundivided. I think about the ones I met across various years through digitalundivided.

There are so many founder stories. I think about digitalundivided founders who have become team members, such as Aly Nicely, digitalundivided Entrepreneur In Residence, helping to lead and give perspective to program participants. Aly was in the position before I became CEO, but I already knew her as CEO of BEAUTY IN COLOR, a company that she built while participating in digitalundivided's BIG program. I got to work with her in a different capacity, see her maturity as an entrepreneur, and how she gives feedback to others.

Since I wrote *The Path Redefined*, there have been so many dots that have been connected. I am now in this moment of realization where there's oddly been a change of control in something I feel I built. It isn't mine, yet I transformed it. And in many ways it's transformed me and allowed me to finally put together my vision and see all the ways that women of color can really level up.

It's not just about leveling up for themselves but how they can build bigger and better businesses. How visibility can change the game. How investment can change the game. How a sound strategy from best-in-class minds, combined with the ability to work in a lean start-up method, can change the game.

It's about how wealth strategies can change the game. How so much in your life can change. How so much in my life has changed in the past three years.

I also never would've imagined that Walmart would call me back. Not after all the people I worked with at the highest levels had already moved on. Janey's gone now. Ben-Saba Hassan, Chief Diversity Officer, is gone. All the Walmart bigwigs I was talking to, who were recruiting me and in my Rolodex, are no longer at the world's largest company. But the world's largest company is still interested in me and people that have joined since my conversations have ended say my reputation very positively precedes me within the company.

People know my name because apparently I left that much of an impression on the executive team that did remain, or the supporting team, full of senior executives who have now been elevated to even higher levels of global leadership. They remember my involvement and contributions on the board.

I think this is all now part of the new version of *The Path Redefined*. I've learned new lessons that have brought mature thinking to my personal life and helped to evolve my professional life. Running something small created a bigger impact than maybe I would have if I had gone to the Fortune 1 at that time.

Would I have been able to see out my vision this quickly, this boldly at Walmart? I don't know. Would building out my vision at Walmart have validated what I've been able to validate in the last two and a half, almost three years, both as CEO of digitalundivided but also just as Lauren Maillian? My own investments, things that have nothing to do with digitalundivided, have also been transformative for me in the last few years. My entire life has changed.

Ruggable, one of my earliest investments, became a unicorn company. I have had the opportunity to invest in new companies that are trending incredibly well and have exits that could be nine figures. These are all things that we've never seen before; I've never had these opportunities. So I think that, yes, digitalundivided was something small that net-net had a really big impact because Lauren went in and did what she always did. She just didn't realize that she's always done it.

I did it with Sugarleaf Vineyards. I have done it with LMB Group, working with top-tier clients throughout the past twelve years. I did it with Gen Y Capital. I have done it with my own investment portfolio and taking a bigger bet than most would've in the Athena SPAC, which announced a successful, nearly one-billion-dollar combination to take public an electric vehicle company in what is arguably the most important tech sector right now, accomplishing what 600 other SPACs in the market couldn't do successfully.

While we won in execution, it's been a tough market and performance for electric vehicles hasn't been easy. It's not ended up as successful or lucrative given my massive six-figure investment, but I gained a billion dollars-plus worth of experience that can't be taken away or replicated, especially not by someone who looks like me, in my circumstances, or at my age.

As a part of my gratitude practice, I constantly remind myself that I am already so much further than I expected, because statistically, I shouldn't be here, or at these tables, or ringing opening bells to take companies public at thirty-eight years old where I invested my own hard-earned money. I am a woman of faith. I walk by faith, not by sight, every day, knowing that I've already broken generational curses and set new standards of possibility.

It's been eleven years since writing *The Path Redefined*, but so much has happened steadily through years one to seven, and in an accelerated fashion the last years of this decade-long stretch. To even look around me in my home and see how my art collection has evolved in the past five years, it is all beyond what I ever imagined. I literally went from buying Pier 1 art to invitation-only pre-auction at Sotheby's and VIP preview access to Art Basel, and I've done it too in the asset classification of art. Works I've collected in the last five years have my collection up seven times in value.

This is the moment about finally being forced to slow down. This is about being forced to be good to myself. I've left digitalundivided under astonishing circumstances when I stood firm in my worth and my value. I always say terms matter more than money.

I had hired innovative talent primarily from companies like Goldman Sachs, Amazon, Intuit, Comcast, ABC, who helped to create the strategic plan of where we saw the organization going in the next three years. The coach and consultant that guided us during this process said to me: "Lauren, I don't know what this is but it isn't an ordinary nonprofit; you've created a new framework."

I realized that while it is a nonprofit, it's just an innovative one. We've received grant monies; we've received some corporate partnership sponsorship dollars. We give out grants, we do impact work, we conduct research, we conduct programs, we engineer programs that close access, opportunity, skill gaps, knowledge gaps for Black and Latina women who are entrepreneurs and innovators. How are we not an ordinary nonprofit? How does this not look like an ordinary nonprofit to you?

She goes: "I don't know. I've just never seen a nonprofit like this before, there's no "lack" mentality."

I'll never forget her saying that to me. There's no "lack" mentality here.

About a year ago, I had a founder conversation where they advised me that they thought their nonprofit company was going to be moving away from entrepreneurship because it was no longer impacting poverty. It was really moving more to the wealth sector. And that wealth creation is not necessarily a charitable cause, but that job creation and skill-building areas are charitable work.

Now that women of color and these underserved communities are beginning to have million-dollar-type outcomes, it looks more like wealth creation than it does job creation or addressing poverty by way of business creation via entrepreneurship. See, even the nonprofit world and its founders were forced to embrace *The Path Redefined*—this entrepreneurial life keeps changing, as do markets, causes, and opportunities.

That's why I always lean on my foundational experience of brand-building and creating conversations that accelerate and amplify—after all, that's what's made me an award-winning marketer. I bring this skill and perspective to everything I do. Sitting at home during the pandemic, watching guys in Silicon Valley wear hoodies and make billions, while leading this nonprofit organization where I was helping women of color raise $50,000 to $1 million, on average, for their companies, while my own investment portfolio grew in unexpected ways made me think . . . We need a new list. One people pay attention to. One that makes people talk. But just like the Forbes, Fortune, and Inc. 5000 lists, one that turns visibility into money for founders who look like me and definitely couldn't wear a hoodie and be taken seriously, let alone raise money in sweats! I brought the idea of *The New C-Suite* to my dear friend Nancy Berger, then Group Publisher at Hearst, and we immediately partnered to make this list a reality—to redefine what a future start-up founder and CEO could look like and to get the world accustomed to that person maybe being a woman of color.

Four years later and my brainchild of a recognition list still lives on in *Cosmopolitan* magazine, minting ten women each year who have doors opened for them and receive inbound interest that didn't exist before. I wanted to create a roadmap for *The Path Redefined* for them too. Thankfully, Nancy and Hearst Magazines validated that. More growth as a marketer who proved the ability to create social change through marketing—the "no lack mentality" really started making more sense to me now. But I'm also not in the business of sitting still. Having experienced the feeling of lack for much of my life, I now subscribe to abundance for me and for you!

I knew there would always be people who couldn't or wouldn't understand a more innovative approach to running a nonprofit. Just like people questioned why I was creating a C-suite honoree list as a nonprofit, some wondered why I partnered with a media company like *Cosmo*. But I knew that this partnership was indeed charitable. By working with Cosmo, we're giving founders valuable exposure and not asking for anything in return, all while helping to transform their businesses.

This work sparked a fire in me to move some of my investing work to a venture studio. I could see how impactful my approach could be with more capital to invest directly in their companies. So maybe that's what Lauren Maillian should do next. Lauren Maillian should go and innovate again as an entrepreneur and start a venture studio because maybe that's what being at digitalundivided was meant to spark for me. And that is when I changed the meaning of LMB Group, my thirteen-year-old company, to Leverage Momentum Build. That's what I do, for companies and brands, for myself and my family, for life and others and for you. I want you to leverage momentum and build—it's the true essence of *The Path Redefined* on repeat. I would only add, don't stop.

Everything that I've been doing in my own little pillar, giving back for the culture and focusing on Black and Latina women at digitalundivided, investing my own money from my own pockets into early-stage start-ups, my own savings, my own investment upside from liquidity events and exits that happened for me in the pandemic . . . maybe everything led me to this moment to really stand up.

In 2022, at an event in New Orleans that I created for the Nasdaq Foundation called InvestHER, I was in conversation with my former mentee, turned dear friend Jewel Burks. When I asked her what made her start Collab Capital, she told me: "My mom looked at me and said, 'Enough writing your own checks, you've done enough now.'"

Now, I think Lauren Maillian is in a similar place. I've hit a really high level for myself, at least at my age, and with the expectations that I had for myself, I've exceeded my wildest dreams and goals.

Looking from the outside, it's easy to think I've had a perfect life, and it's no surprise because you can screw me over (and punch me in the face), but I'm going to look fabulous while it happens. So many people don't know my hurdles and heartaches because I just had to make it, and I had no choice but to make it work.

It may seem like my life is perfect, with all the traveling, successful businesses, and high-profile brand collaborations. However, while I'm not always at ease discussing the difficulties I've faced, these hardships are a significant part of my entrepreneurial journey and success story, and I feel they need to be shared.

Also, the difference between where you are now and where you want to be may lie in the lessons you draw from my lived experience. I want people like me to understand the setbacks I've faced as a woman and as a person of color and to realize that you have the power to determine the direction of your career, no matter your current struggles.

When I walked out of an abusive marriage and became a single mother to two kids under the age of two at just twenty-four, I felt it was the only thing people saw. Now, with nearly grown, responsible teens who lack nothing and a wonderful husband, those eight and a half years as a single mom were incredibly challenging but toughened me up into the Lauren you now know. I was the sole financial provider for my children, never receiving a dime in child support up until this day.

When you see Lauren Maillian, you see someone who created everything for herself: no silver spoon, no trust fund, no inherited wealth. It was all sheer grit and determination. So if no one ever handed you anything and you don't see anyone coming to save you, know that you can save yourself. It is possible. I did it. There is always a way to turn things in your favor. And I've done that since I was a child.

> So if no one ever handed you anything and you don't see anyone coming to save you, know that you can save yourself.

As a little girl many years ago, I had a lemonade and iced tea stand on the corner of 96th Street and Madison Avenue, across from where I grew up. For four consecutive summers—from eight to twelve—I ran my stand, selling two sizes of drinks. I quickly realized it was too hot to set up on a random corner in the Manhattan summer sun, so I struck a deal with the owners of Jerome Florists to use their shaded awning. In exchange, I paid them $50 a week. Despite my low prices, I constantly pulled in $300 a day in sales. Before I turned ten, I had my first taste of entrepreneurial success. While my friends depended on allowances from their parents, I was independent and making real money.

This independent, take-charge attitude led me to start an independent modeling career at age six. I modeled for top agencies in New York, London, Paris, and Los Angeles until I was eighteen. At nineteen, I started a vineyard that soon became a successful winery while working toward my undergraduate degree and starting my family.

In 2011, I was selected for the *Empact 100 List* at twenty-six, recognizing the top one hundred American entrepreneurs under thirty. This honor took me to the White House for an awards ceremony, where I spoke about the importance of entrepreneurship and giving back.

In 2016, my media career took off with a spot on the TV show *Quit Your Day Job* on Oxygen (NBCU). It seemed like the perfect opportunity to share my entrepreneurial insights with a broader audience. But as the season progressed, the channel's focus shifted, and the show was not renewed. This was a hard pill to swallow. I had invested so much time, energy, and resources, only to see it end prematurely. Despite the disappointment, it taught me valuable lessons about the unpredictability of success.

In 2019, I joined Walmart's Board of Disruptors, bringing my entrepreneurial insights to one of the world's largest retail corporations. In 2020, I became CEO of digitalundivided, an organization focused on economic empowerment for women of color through innovation and entrepreneurship. This role allowed me to make a meaningful impact on a community I deeply care about.

In 2021, I launched *The New C-Suite* in partnership with *Cosmopolitan*, redefining modern leadership with a focus on diversity and inclusion. In 2022, I launched the InvestHER Power Series with the Nasdaq Foundation, supporting female entrepreneurs with resources and mentorship.

In 2023, I served as a judge for the Cartier Women's Initiative, culminating in an inspiring award ceremony in Paris. I also became President of Digital Innovation at Hero Media and a jury member for the Effie Awards US in the same year.

Most of these achievements are likely what you will find with a simple search of who Lauren Maillian is and what she has accomplished. However, what you won't find is that I have felt lost at delicate points in my life. I have missed opportunities and had to humbly admit that I wasn't good enough for them at the time. I have felt alone, abandoned, and betrayed by those I trusted the most. I have failed many times. And I have feared for myself, my children, and my future more times than I can count.

My entrepreneurial path is intertwined with personal struggles and triumphs, shaping who I am today. Each setback and success has been a stepping stone, teaching me resilience and determination. By sharing my story, I hope to inspire others to see that no matter the challenges, there is always a way forward. You have the power to shape your own destiny, just as I have shaped mine.

MAILLIAN

WHAT I'VE LEARNED ABOUT BUSINESS

Stacy Francis is the President and CEO of Francis Financial, a fee-only boutique wealth management, financial planning, and divorce financial planning firm dedicated to providing ongoing comprehensive advice for successful individuals, couples, and women in transition, such as divorce or widowhood.

She is a great example of a woman who built a business rooted in her core expertise. She attained success on her own terms as an entrepreneur while simultaneously creating a legacy of financial success for others. Here's her advice on business:

1. Choose a path that you're passionate about. It will keep you energized and focused through good times and bad.

2. Remember that the vast majority of successful people have achieved their success through hard work. Talent and intelligence, though important, are, in my belief, secondary to hard work and consistent commitment to your goals and career path.

3. As an employer/manager, never forget the value of your staff. Having a good team and showing them that they're appreciated will pay dividends in terms of your long-term success.

4. I believe that sheer grit has contributed the most to my success. By grit I'm referring to my ability to bounce back from setbacks and hardship and stay committed to helping my clients each and every day.

My mother and father had a huge influence on my entrepreneurial journey. When my parents divorced, my mom was forced to reinvent herself—and boy, did she. She became the director of corporate public relations at *Essence* magazine, where she was a key member of the leadership team. I saw her as a powerful and influential woman in a male-dominated business arena. I didn't see her cooking and cleaning, I saw her hustling and multitasking—then hitting the red carpet at night.

My father was a tough and successful investment banker who made sure I knew that there were no guarantees in life and that I would have to work hard for anything I wanted. Because of his influence, I knew from an early age how to run a business or at least what it looked like. I was never formally taught these necessary skills, but I did hang out at my parents' offices doing homework after school, and I soaked up everything I could, especially when I participated in the Take Our Daughters and Sons to Work activities. I had different goals, dreams, and aspirations than the other children I knew. I wanted to go to work each day, attend board meetings and take the train to Washington, DC, for powerful business trips like my father had done throughout my childhood.

MAILLIAN: YOUR PROFESSIONAL LIFE

You control whether you sink or swim by relying on logic, but ultimately, I trust my intuition and confidently march to the beat of my own drum.

I always wanted to be big. In fact, my favorite film growing up was *Big* (1988), which starred Tom Hanks as Josh, a twelve-year-old boy who becomes a thirty-year-old man overnight (though still with his twelve-year-old brain and personality). Josh is hired by a toy company where he is quickly promoted to an executive position because of his unique insight on what children really want. I imagined myself as Josh, participating in important meetings and having the ear of all the adults in the room.

In some ways, I was able to be like Josh. Beginning at age twelve, I was fortunate to work at some of America's top businesses. I interned at *Essence* magazine for its CFO, Harry Dedyo, and I worked with The Terrie Williams Agency—a leading public relations and communications firm, and supported Rachel Noerdlinger, who is now one of the most powerful public relations experts in the country. I spent my summers interning with college students, and I loved it.

I grew up in a world filled with successful and powerful men and women, and I wanted to be like them. But I knew that the success I envisioned for my own future was never guaranteed and I couldn't take it for granted. I knew that I would have to work hard to find the success I desired in life, and when I found that success, I would have to work hard to find new opportunities and new successes.

So work I did, and work I will.

When I participated in the White House ceremony honoring the *Empact 100* young entrepreneurs in 2011, I made a pledge to give back and pay it forward. I will have accomplished that goal if readers gain a newfound confidence that allows them to recalibrate how they look at success and live their lives on their own terms. The entrepreneurial journey is one of the most empowering, thrilling, and rewarding things anyone can experience in life. Being able to do what you love and to be successful at it is truly a gift.

Before you read another page, please answer the following questions for yourself: Who are you the cumulative investment of? Who has believed in you? Take a few minutes to write a thank you note to those important people in your life because far too many people don't. I have personally written numerous thank you notes because I am the result of the cumulative investment of the many people who've believed in me throughout my life, and the many people who've believed in me throughout my life, and who saw more opportunity for me than I could see, and I know that I will write many more in the future. In fact, I look forward to it.

You are also the cumulative investment of the many people who have believed in you throughout your life. I hope that you learn from my own experiences as an entrepreneur, mother, and a forty-year-old woman, and that you are able to apply and leverage these lessons for yourself, whether you use them in business or in your personal life. They have worked for me, and there's no reason that they can't work for you, too.

LESSONS I HAVE LEARNED

- Redefining your path requires you to take the uncommon route and embrace risks at what might seem to be the least logical time.

- Create breakthrough moments in your life by being prepared for, and by attracting, opportunities from many different sources.

- Keep growing by always learning and always experiencing new things.

- Learn to work around obstacles instead of being trapped by them.

- Be interesting—create the kind of appeal that transcends age, experience, race, and culture and will make you a well-rounded and meaningful addition to any team or company.

- If your dreams don't scare you, they aren't big enough. Remember: they should always be worth it, even if you fall.

I have made my biggest, boldest bets with my own money, just as I did with Sugarleaf Vineyards, which had no outside funding—just as I've always done. I think maybe it is time to institutionalize it a little bit. Maybe it is time for Lauren Maillian to go out and raise money to bring all of these pillars of supporting founders by giving platform services, visibility, storytelling services, and incubating their brands. Not necessarily with programs.

I think that digitalundivided sparked for me the idea that there is a model in which I can help founders through advisory or creating a framework combined with visibility and storytelling to build platforms to connect their dots, introduce them to the right partners, the right retailers, and the right opportunities.

I've proven my investment prowess from angel investment deals throughout the years. I worked with Perspective Equity Partners on a one hundred million dollar deal for Camille Rose, where I learned how to understand private equity and how to maximize resources, create leverage, cut casts, drive profitability, and ultimately acquire a company in operation so that I knew how to do it whenever I wanted to do it again.

I've proven I can take huge risks but also deliver great rewards, just like I did with digitalundivided. In less than two years, I increased our revenue by five times, grew our team exponentially and got more than five billion media impressions through initiatives like *The New C-Suite* and Project Diane.

As a thought leader, my ideas, opinions, and perspectives have always centered around driving parity and increasing the valuation of work aimed at closing the wealth and opportunity gaps for women of color in the tech and innovation sectors. While digitalundivided was dedicated to supporting Black and Latina women specifically, my commitment extends far beyond these communities.

I am deeply invested in creating opportunities for all those who have been overlooked or counted out, including men and individuals from diverse backgrounds. As a mother to a Black son, I am acutely aware of the challenges faced by Black men as well. My mission has always been to foster success for women of color in tech and innovation, but it also includes a broader vision of equality and support for everyone who has been marginalized.

2

My Life Is
Serendipitous by Design

YOU'RE PROBABLY WONDERING BY NOW exactly
what I mean by that. It means that although I try not to plan
every detail in my life, I ensure that I'm in the right place at the right
time to enable good things to happen.

It's no accident that I have a great network of people and many
opportunities have developed from this network. I am still in touch
with, and friends with, the people I looked up to, interned for, and
worked with more than ten, even twenty-plus, years ago. I used to
wonder why I would meet such amazing people at different events
I attended. It must surely be a remarkable coincidence that they
happened to be at the same place I was. Eventually, I realized that it
wasn't remarkable at all; we were traveling within the same networks
and circles of business and social colleagues and acquaintances. These

meetings were serendipitous, but they were not accidentally attended and I was prepared for them.

As a little girl, I dreamed about doing mortgage-backed acquisitions. I'm serious. I wanted to be an investment banker like my father. If there's one recurring theme throughout my life, it's that I wanted to be powerful and I wanted to be big and I wanted to be successful. As an entrepreneur, most of the businesses I started were on my own or with a small team.

It's therefore not surprising that I never played a team sport ever. My love was individual sports, the kind that depended solely on how well I performed as a player and not on how well my team did. I tried field hockey for a second, and I failed miserably at basketball. In fact, when I dropped out of basketball, I decided to run the scoreboard for the guys' and girls' teams.

Lauren

MAILLIAN: SERENDIPITY

Follow a general path but stay open to the possibility of unexpected opportunities appearing along the way. Always be prepared for the next big opportunity whenever it may arise. Know the resources you need and be committed to quickly learning what you need to know to be successful.

The one activity that I always stuck with was the violin. I was good at it, and according to my father, the violin is great for people who are mathematicians. He's always thought that I was a number and math whiz. I also thrived as an equestrian, and it was the focus of my life for some time to the point where, when I was in school, I got special permission to use my hours of horseback riding as my PE credit and began training for the Olympics.

I thrived on having control over my destiny. For as long as I can remember, I have wanted to take personal responsibility for my life. I thrive on the knowledge that I'm responsible for my successes and failures. No one else. Whether or not I achieve it is all on me. This is what drives me, and this has always been my personality.

So while I have put myself in positions where good outcomes have resulted for me in business, I haven't made a habit of planning out each step along the way. Instead, I follow a general path and stay open to the possibility of unexpected opportunities appearing along the way. Sugarleaf Vineyards was a real estate investment that I turned into a business. There was no big plan to create Luxury Market Branding. It came about when my network found out I was moving on from the vineyard, and many brands voiced their need for my marketing and branding savvy within their companies. I didn't realize that I wanted my next venture to be in marketing and branding, but that was where my expertise and the needs of my network collided—it was the opportunity of the moment that made the most sense and would yield the best results.

After I sold my interest in the winery, I was ready to get out of the business world for a while and enjoy my children. But Selena Cuffe, founder of the Los Angeles-based Heritage Link Brands and one of my first clients, challenged this idea. I can clearly remember what she said to me. "What do you mean you're just going to hang out with your kids? Absolutely not. You've got the chops to do something else."

So I began Luxury Market Branding. As I was growing that company, I started getting really involved in angel investing—a term meaning when someone provides capital to a start-up usually in exchange for equity in the company. I soon found myself advising a small group of start-ups in New York City.

I have always been a detail-oriented planner with a keen eye for how my businesses should operate and improve. I'm all about efficiency in every sense of the word. I want to get it right and keep it moving so that I can tackle the next issue at hand. Then wash, rinse, and repeat until I dramatically exceed what others believed to have been possible.

This personal approach makes sense when you consider that wineries are one of the top ten most highly regulated industries in the country. I was able to fly through all the arduous paperwork and process, and I had a real skill for forming companies and overseeing logistics, management, and operations. But not only did I have the business chops required for success, I also had the right personality. If nothing else. I'm hardworking, committed, innovative, passionate, and energetic. I was the kind of person that my colleagues turned to when they faced a challenge or found an opportunity.

That's what led me to help begin Gen Y Capital Partners. I was extremely interested and intrigued about what was going on in the venture, start-up, and technology landscapes happening here in New York City, but also in Silicon Valley and the rest of the country. What I found particularly intriguing about start-ups and venture funds is that the pace was completely different than what I was used to with my winery. It took my money, money from my savings and previous investments to get the winery up and running, and then years of waiting while I watched the grapes grow, built a building, pressed the grapes, made the wine, and then bottled it. It was a dream greatly deferred.

In contrast, technology start-ups are sprouting everywhere all the time, and they can be in business within weeks and profitable within months. This was amazing to me, and I was extremely interested. And so that deeply passionate interest in the start-up and venture world, combined with my proven business skills, led me to immerse myself in the industry and find success pursuing my new passion. I wanted to do everything better than I had seen it done before. I thought a better way was possible.

So, yes, my life really is serendipitous, and some great opportunities have come my way, but they happen because of the way that I integrate my work life with my personal life. Consider how I started Gen Y Capital Partners. I began the fund with people I met about a year before through an entrepreneurship organization. We weren't working together at the time, but we realized that we could start a business together and Gen Y Capital Partners was born.

After the business was up and running, I spent a long time asking myself, "Now, how exactly did that happen? Was it that the right people were all at the right place at the right time?"

BUILD A LIFE THAT IS SERENDIPITOUS BY DESIGN

Now I realize that the company was no accident. I didn't plan it, but there was some design involved. It came about because of the people I chose to surround myself with and because of the networks that I have created throughout every facet of my life.

Think about your own life for a moment, and ask yourself the following questions:

- ▶ What are you doing to make your life serendipitous by design?
- ▶ Who's in your network?
- ▶ Who are you having lunch with next week?
- ▶ What events are you attending?
- ▶ Who would you like to meet that you haven't yet done so?

▶ In what business networks and social circles do these people spend their time, and how can you become a part of them?

Your reputation within your network is priceless. Anyone who tells you that they don't think about what someone else thinks of them isn't being truthful. Opinions and impressions matter whether we like it or not.

A point worth clarifying since the term "networking" is overused and shrouded in jargon more often than not: Do not social climb. It is, generally speaking, very obvious, immature, and almost always tacky and disingenuous. However, learning to socialize intelligently will change the game of how you operate and are perceived by others. When you learn to socialize intelligently, you prove that you are thoughtful, insightful, and smart. As a result, the relationships you accumulate in your career will reflect the approach you took to nurturing and growing your network in a sincere way that provides reciprocal value.

Don't daydream. Strategize how you're going to execute the vision of your dreams. Believe me, if I can do this, then so can you and so can anyone.

After a decade of new experiences, there are seven lessons guiding me in this next chapter of my life.

LESSON 1

FAMILY OVER EVERYTHING

I've always known this to be true but didn't always live by it. I am guilty of spending more time working and chasing achievements than being with the ones I love the most. It's an interesting paradox: I love them so much that I never want them to lack anything. I've worked really hard to navigate the unexpected hurdles in life that could have set me back, but now, I've sprung forward and am where I hoped to be at fifty.

The most beautiful lesson from my family's move to Puerto Rico has been diving into a culture where it's always family over everything. I'm so grateful to this island and its people for teaching me to slow down, enjoy those who mean the most to me, and find the beauty in redefining success while prioritizing family. I was working so hard that I missed too many important moments with them, but luckily, it's not too late.

Raising my children on my own since they were just babies has been a journey filled with both immense challenges and indescribable joys. We've only had each other, and the pain of neglect during my relentless pursuit of success in my years of single motherhood is something I never want any of them to ever experience. It has also strengthened our bond in ways I could never have imagined. Every setback, every struggle, has reinforced my resolve to give Jayden and Chloe the best life possible.

Finding love again has been a beautiful twist in our story. My children now have a dad who fills the role so well, offering them the love and support I always dreamed they would have. Seeing them bond, laugh, and create new memories together has been the greatest reward. The first time I saw Jayden and Chloe run into his arms with joy, I knew that all the sacrifices and heartaches were worth it. Our family feels complete in a way I never thought possible, and it has made me even more committed to being present for them.

LESSON 2

ONE-ON-ONE CONNECTIONS WITH YOUR CHILDREN

One of the most important lessons I've learned over the years is the irreplaceable value of spending one-on-one time with my children. The highlight of the past few years for me and my children was the dedicated time we spent together, nurturing our bond, and creating lasting memories.

In a study of 14,000 U.S. children, researchers found that 40 percent lack strong emotional bonds with their parents—bonds that are crucial for success later in life. What some parents may not realize is the ripple effect that strong emotional bonds can have on their children's development and future success.

> I'm glad I learned this lesson early on—you can always make more money, land more clients, grow more businesses, but you can never get lost time back.

I'm glad I learned this lesson early on—you can always make more money, land more clients, grow more businesses, but you can never get lost time back. So I spend quality time strengthening the connection I have with my children because I can never have lost time back. Chloe will never be fourteen again, and Jayden will never be sixteen again.

My eldest, Jayden, turned sixteen this past year. To celebrate this milestone, we dedicated time to just the two of us. We started his birthday with a special breakfast, sharing stories and laughter. Then, we took a golf cart ride, where we got into deeper conversations about life, his dreams, and his goals. These moments were an opportunity to connect on a profound level.

Jayden, who has always shown incredible foresight and maturity, has been my rock since he was young. I recall him reassuring me during tough times as a single mother, saying, "Mama, it's gonna be okay." And he was right.

In 2024 we had a remarkable experience that emphasized the importance of these connections. I had the privilege of taking my children with me to the Cannes Lions International Festival of Creativity for the second time. This trip was not just about attending a prestigious event but also about exposing them to new cultures and experiences. Walking the red carpet with my children by my side was a surreal moment. It allowed us to share the excitement of my professional achievements and blend them seamlessly with family life.

This summer, we embarked on a family tour around Europe, a journey that brought us even closer together. We explored historic sites, tasted diverse cuisines, and embraced the rich cultural heritage of each country we visited. From the bustling streets of Paris to the serene canals of Venice, each destination offered unique experiences that we cherished as a family. These adventures not only broadened our horizons but also reinforced the importance of being present and creating memories together.

When I immerse myself fully in their world, I see them thrive. They open up about their fears, dreams, and even the small details of their daily lives. I see how these shared experiences deepen our bond, and I understand the significance of being present.

I've come to realize that the true essence of parenting lies in these moments. Making time for the little things, being present, and showing our children that they are valued. Through these experiences, I've learned that quality time is not just a gift to my children but a gift to myself as well. It allows me to understand them better, support them more effectively, and cherish the joy they bring into my life.

In every one-on-one interaction, whether it's a simple conversation over breakfast, a grand adventure in Cannes, or a family tour around Europe, I find the strength and inspiration to be the best mother I can be. Because while my professional achievements are significant, the love and connection I share with my children are what truly define success.

LESSON 3

TERMS MATTER MORE THAN MONEY

We've grown up in a world and been surrounded by images of success that tell us money and a dollar figure are the ultimate pinnacles. However, the terms and conditions matter more than anything. There comes a point in life and business where money simply isn't enough, especially if the terms are set up for you to fail. This is a lesson in all aspects of life and something that the founders and high-achieving women I mentor know best. The money might seem great at first, but if the terms are set up to make you fail, you must make the best decision for yourself. This is when we realize that money isn't everything.

I often encounter similar situations. Many of the women I work with are offered deals that seem promising financially but come with terms that could set them up for failure. I emphasize to them that money, while important, should not be the sole factor in their decision-making process.

One mentee, a brilliant entrepreneur, was offered an investment that could have significantly accelerated her company's growth. However, the terms included relinquishing a large portion of control over her business. Through our discussions, she realized that maintaining control and preserving her vision were paramount. She declined the offer and later secured a better deal that aligned with her values and allowed her to retain control.

This lesson also applies to personal decisions. Understanding that terms matter more than money is recognizing your worth and maintaining integrity, setting boundaries, and knowing when to walk away from a situation that doesn't serve your best interests. This principle has guided me through numerous professional and personal challenges, ensuring that I make decisions that align with my values and long-term goals.

LESSON 4

THE POWER OF SAYING NO

One of the most valuable lessons I've learned in my journey is the power of saying no. This lesson has played a crucial role in helping me identify opportunities that truly align with my vision and propel my career forward.

Throughout my career, I've received numerous offers to join media companies, start-ups, and funds. While these opportunities often seemed promising on the surface, a deeper examination revealed misalignments with my personal and professional values.

For instance, many offers came with goals and objectives that seemed skewed. The work required was often unfairly balanced in ways that did not reflect the partnership and compensation structure. I was often asked to do so much for so little, and that's never been okay with me. I believe in fair compensation for the value I bring, and compromising on this principle would have only led to resentment and burnout.

Moreover, I've had doubts about the teams behind these opportunities. Whether it was the founding team, the future team, or the integrity of their past projects, these uncertainties played a significant role in my decision-making process. I've learned that a great idea is only as good as the people executing it. If the team doesn't work well together or lacks integrity, the project is likely to fail, regardless of how promising it may seem initially.

Timing is another critical factor. There have been instances where the timing just wasn't right for me to seize some really exciting opportunities. Balancing multiple responsibilities, both personal and professional, means that sometimes, despite the allure of a new venture, the timing just doesn't align with my current commitments.

Resources, or the lack thereof, also influence my decisions. There have been times when the resources available were insufficient to accomplish the work expected. Unrealistic timetables were another frequent issue. While I pride myself on being efficient, I don't believe in rushing to build something of value. Quality takes time, and I am not willing to compromise on that.

Finally, many people have approached me, thinking I would be the magic wand to make everything happen. While I appreciate their confidence in my abilities, that burden felt too much on my shoulders alone. Excitement and passion for the work are essential, but it's equally important to be realistic about what can be achieved. Building something of value requires a dedicated and collaborative effort, not just one person carrying the entire load.

The power of saying no has allowed me to stay true to my values, maintain my integrity, and ensure that every opportunity I pursue is genuinely worth my time and effort. This lesson has been pivotal in my journey, helping me to prioritize what truly matters and enabling me to build a career that aligns with my vision and aspirations.

LESSON 5

ALWAYS ASSUME GOOD INTENT

Working in diversity, equity, inclusion, and belonging (DEIB) over the past two and a half years, and becoming a leader in social impact, I've learned that many of the issues and conversations we face are inherently uncomfortable. Assuming good intent is particularly powerful because it allows us to navigate difficult conversations with empathy and openness, creating a space where true understanding and change can occur.

This lesson stems from the realization that we don't always need to be on the defensive. This may not be the easiest thing to do as a Black woman constantly treated like a misfit or as a non-minority woman who has always felt overlooked or is navigating unexpected life changes. Often, how you respond to these questions can set the tone for how a relationship or opportunity will unfold.

When you've felt like the underdog, constantly needing to prove your worth, it can be difficult to let your guard down. But there comes a point when you need to flip the switch, to stop fighting and simply show why you're amazing. Assuming good intent means believing that people are often just curious and may lack the tact or knowledge to approach certain topics delicately. What might come across as offensive, condescending, or stereotyping is often not malicious but rather a product of broader circumstances.

Unless someone has blatantly shown otherwise, their questions usually come from a place of genuine curiosity. So, shift your focus to why you deserve to be in the room, why you belong, instead of spending your energy on the tone or tenor with which a conversation began. This perspective allows you to engage more openly and constructively, paving the way for more productive and positive interactions.

SELF-CARE PRACTICES

There is power in learning how to quiet your mind and decrease your own stress levels, especially when you are in a position of leadership. As a CEO, a founder, and mother, I have found comfort and confidence in designing a routine that prioritizes my self-care, including my nutrition, meditations, and workouts. We all deserve that.

Self-care has always been important to me, but it has truly evolved over the past eight to ten years. My approach to working out has undergone a significant transformation. In my modeling days, I considered working out to be walking on a 3 percent incline on the treadmill for thirty minutes at a pace of three or four miles per hour. Back then, my goal wasn't to be strong or toned; it was simply to stay slim enough to maintain a career as a highly paid model.

As a model, my primary objective was to meet the literal measurements expected of me on my composite card, which always included my measurements in inches and centimeters. Working out was pure cardio to keep up with these measurements, allowing me to earn a living that would later enable me to invest in real estate, a vineyard, start-ups, and more.

During that time, the Atkins diet was all the rage, emphasizing high fat and low carbs. My diet now, however, is vastly different. I focus on high protein, leafy greens, and take a variety of natural, non-GMO, organic supplements tailored to my specific needs. These include omega-3s, women's vitamins, chlorophyll, spirulina, GABA, and maca. Instead of coffee, I drink herbal tea, having long since given up coffee with hazelnut creamer.

Even on days when I can't get a rigorous workout, I make it a point to stretch or walk around the city. This past summer, while traveling around Europe, I kept up with my steps even if I wasn't following my usual workout routine. My definition of being active and my approach to self-care have completely changed. Given the increased stress, responsibility, and senior roles I now hold, this evolution was necessary.

My life now involves juggling multiple roles as a mom, a wife, a founder of several companies, an investor, and a mentor to other companies and founders. Managing my personal brand, writing, overseeing my thought leadership, social media, my children's homework and college applications, and their social-emotional health and well-being requires a level of self-care far beyond what was necessary twenty years ago.

In the past, my main responsibilities were to be on time, kind, and prepared—largely by meeting specific measurements. Today, my daily routine involves drinking a gallon of water, adhering to a balanced diet, and engaging in comprehensive wellness practices to meet the expectations of my mind and body. This holistic approach to self-care allows me to show up and perform at the high level required by my current roles.

LESSON 7

THE DIFFERENCE BETWEEN BEING A FOUNDER AND CEO VS. JUST BEING CEO

There's a significant difference between building something from scratch as a founder and CEO and stepping into a leadership role as a CEO of an existing organization. Each path offers unique challenges and opportunities, and understanding these distinctions can greatly impact how you approach your role and lead effectively.

One of the key lessons I've learned is that, as CEO, whether you're a founder or not, your primary responsibility is to lead with vision and integrity—and lead you must.

When I built my first company at nineteen, I was deeply intertwined with the very essence of my organization. I've been there from the inception, nurturing the idea, shaping the vision, and laying the foundation brick by brick. The connection to the company was visceral; it was my baby, my creation. A very similar feeling I share as the CEO and founder of LMB Group. Having the freedom to create and innovate from the ground up, setting the culture, the values, and the mission, and being the driving force behind every strategic decision, every hire, and every pivot, the pressure to succeed can be immense because the stakes are so personal.

In contrast, stepping into the role of a CEO in a company you didn't found—case in point, my past role as CEO at digitalundivided—presents a different set of dynamics. Your challenge is to lead, innovate, and drive growth within the framework that already exists. This requires a different kind of skill set—one that balances respect for the existing structure with the ability to implement meaningful change.

3

Make No Small Plans

(Don't Just Wing It)

F OR EVERY SUCCESSFUL MAN OR woman, there
are plenty of others who, for some reason or another, don't make
it. The reasons for failure in business—and in life—are many. In fact,
when you run down the list of possible problems, obstacles, and
missed opportunities, you'd think it's a miracle that anyone succeeds
at all. But succeed they do.

And although on some rare occasions, people succeed merely
because they happen to be in the right place at the right time, in my
experience, you've got to *plan* to be a success if you want to *ensure*
that you will be a success. This is true whether you're an entrepreneur
starting up a new venture, a manager in a large corporation hoping
to land a promotion, or an active volunteer in a community-based
organization. *Success is not synonymous with winging it.* Like I said

above, you've got to *plan* for your success, not just *hope* for it. You've also got to be ready for the inevitable failures—see Chapter 14 for more about that.

I have found that one of the most powerful (and as it turns out, one of the simplest) actions you can take to get you on your path to success is to simply set goals. But not any old goals will do. I personally need huge, aspirational goals that excite and motivate me through any ups and downs that I may encounter—they are the light I expect to see at the end of the tunnel. Here's how I approach this task:

- ▶ Find a quiet, comfortable place where I can avoid interruption for an hour or so.

- ▶ Begin to form a picture in my mind of what I want to be doing six months from now, a year from now, five years from now—and where I want to be doing it.

- ▶ Allow my mind to wander without limits and to consider all the possibilities for how I can attain the vision of my future—especially the ones that seem most nearly impossible to attain but with the greatest potential rewards.

- ▶ Choose the one path to the future that gets me most excited and motivated and turn it into an aspirational goal.

- ▶ Set smaller, readily attainable goals that define the exact path I will follow along the way to achieving my aspirational goal. It's not these smaller goals that keep me motivated, however, but more the process of setting the lofty, aspirational goal and then coming as close as I possibly can to achieving it.

I've been responsible for my actions—both the successes and the mistakes—since I was a teenager. I juggled school and a modeling career, achieved grades that made my parents proud, and pulled down the kind of summer income from my lemonade stand that most children only dream of. I learned to negotiate for myself, first as a model negotiating with my agent and ultimately with clients. I next developed an interest in investing in real estate, so I learned how to create plans to turn properties that were depressed into lucrative assets.

MAILLIAN: TAKING RISKS

When pursuing an opportunity, ask yourself, "Will it have been worth it even if I fail?" Once that answer is clearly a resounding "yes," the potential risks morph into rewards, such as acceleration and expansion of business experience.

I know no other way than to thrive under pressure, but I always have a plan about what my end goal is. The plan to get there may not always be as methodical, but the purpose in my journey is clear and my contingency plan if all else fails is even clearer.

I have lost count of the number of times I've talked to someone in the corporate world who's thinking of starting his or her own business. In almost every case, the person thinks that starting a business is going to be easy—come up with a great idea for a new product or service, throw together a website, and wait for those orders to roll in, right? Wrong. The dream is often not as great as the promise. You've got to have the right idea and the right mindset—you've got to think like an entrepreneur. And you've got to have a plan.

When I talk about having a plan, I don't mean that you've got to devote a year of your life to creating a 359-page document that details every single action that you're going to do to build your business and make it run. That's not necessary. When I talk about having a plan, I mean that you've got to have a clear vision of what your business is going to be and then a simple schedule of milestones and benchmarks that you create, even if you're only creating them for yourself.

Having a plan also means that you know and are very clear and comfortable with your personal goals and your non-negotiables, and that any opportunity you accept aligns with those values and furthers your personal goals. My most prominent non-negotiables are:

- Anything that compromises my integrity.

- Not having the level of autonomy that allows me to control the majority of how I schedule my time.

- Inflexibility for an indefinite period of time.

- Lack of complete transparency in a partnership.

- Unclear benchmarks and milestones by which to measure expectations and gauge success.

Don't constantly recalibrate your barometer for success despite all temptations. If you attempt to recalibrate your goals after each accomplishment, your benchmarks will get thrown out of whack and you will never feel proud of the progress you have made and all of the efforts you put forth to make it happen. You'll lose sight of your ultimate goal because your target will keep moving; it will quickly turn into mental warfare and you'll feel like a hamster on a treadmill.

You will slowly but surely frustrate yourself and doubt if the progress you've made is good enough. You must know when to hold out for the right opportunity. Think of your life as an ecosystem— each part has to work to the benefit and betterment of the other.

IDENTIFYING AND ESTABLISHING
YOUR NON-NEGOTIABLES

Non-negotiables are the theoretical underpinning of what enables us to accept responsibility and accountability with ease and joy. You should establish this set of rules, both professionally and personally, to help you maintain your inner compass. These guidelines should motivate you toward bigger and better things, and they should help you achieve happiness and preserve your sanity despite difficult situations. It's important to take the time to establish your list of non-negotiables so you are prepared and resolute when the time comes.

My non-negotiables are the foundations and moral basis for my decisions, and they determine if and how I am incentivized. My non-negotiables are the rules I am not willing to break. They help me maintain the level and type of autonomy that I need to be happy and thrive under the most pressured circumstances.

Everyone's non-negotiables are different. What are yours?

To me, the best entrepreneurs know how to spot an opportunity and understand the value of seizing the moment. They recognize the advantages of being the first to make a move or get in on the deal early and appreciate the importance of adaptability, which is always necessary along the way. However, this doesn't mean you don't need a plan. Opportunities rarely come out of nowhere. It can take many years of hard work, planning, and preparation to be in the right place at the right time so that when that opportunity arises, you'll be able to act on it.

In his book *Outliers: The Story of Success* (Little, Brown and Company, 2008), Malcolm Gladwell presents the idea that to reach the top in your chosen field, you need to devote at least ten thousand hours to that pursuit. Ten thousand hours equates to about five years of full-time practice, laser-focused on a particular skill or area of expertise—or 2.75 years if you're a real go-getter working fifteen-hour days, five days a week, and taking two to three weeks of vacation each year. When you put it in these terms, imagine how many industries you could become an expert in within a single lifetime, excluding, of course, mastering love, parenthood, and the greatest joys of your personal life.

Being prepared to act on an opportunity has nothing to do with luck but everything to do with having the wherewithal—mental, financial, or otherwise—to be ready, willing, and able to act on that opportunity.

No matter how successful you may think you are, the fact is you're always adapting. In his book *The Start-Up of You: Adapt to the Future, Invest in Yourself, and Transform Your Career* (Crown Publishing Group, 2012), LinkedIn founder Reid Hoffman discusses the concept of permanent beta. According to Hoffman, the best entrepreneurial career strategy emphasizes being adaptable and light on your feet while also planning smart. The idea is to choose a market or industry that accounts for your ongoing adaptability.

Existing competitive assets, aspirations, and market needs; launch a thought-out Plan A on a leap of faith; and then systematically experiment and adapt as you accumulate lessons, pivoting to a Plan B as necessary. Entrepreneurs are always a work in progress; they are in permanent beta.

I never know what's going to happen on the other end of a phone call or an email. I always have to be prepared. For years, I had been thinking about starting a business in the beauty industry, but I hadn't found the right opportunity.

In June 2013, my opportunity magnet went into high gear when I met Ido Leffler, co-founder of Yes To Inc., a natural beauty products company that's the number two natural brand in the United States. You can find Yes To products in more than twenty-eight thousand stores in twenty-five countries, including Walmart, Walgreens, and Whole Foods Market.

Ido and I are connected through many of our entrepreneur networks—we have at least fifty colleagues and friends in common—and it was very easy for us to vet each other. We quickly discovered that, for the past couple of years, we had both been thinking about starting a new business—one that would introduce a groundbreaking line of beauty products. Given our mutual interests, we decided to see if we could combine our energies, talents, and networks to create something fun, new, and interesting.

So, I flew to San Francisco, where Yes To Inc. has its headquarters, to meet with Ido. When I arrived, I didn't really know what the plan was for our day other than that it was going to be spent with Ido. We were going to see if we liked each other, if we could make our concept work, and if we could give it life, breath, and vision.

We immediately started discussing creating a line of beauty products for women. Ido and I are real go-getters in every sense of the word, so it didn't take us long to create our list of products. Ido also asked me to create a list of must-haves for myself as a founder and as a woman who knows the market. Soon we were in Union Square doing market research, walking from Bloomingdale's to Target to Walgreens, checking out existing products.

After our market research in Union Square, our next stop was the Yes To Inc. office. Then we headed to lunch and began to map out what this company would look like. We discussed the details of selecting and trademarking a name, moving forward with branding based on that name, and researching the products that we wanted to create and test products that the market really needed.

We asked: What does the market have, not have, and truly need? Where do most women shop? What are the must-have products? We made a list of key roles that we would need for our founding team—the positions and which departments these positions would be in, and then we literally plugged in people from our respective networks that we'd immediately turn to for consultation or full-time employment. We did the same for an advisory board, deciding which perspectives would be of value, as well as the people who could bring them to us. We wrote that down and then made a list of people to reach out to. We talked through our marketing strategy, our distribution strategy—the whole nine yards.

Throughout the day, we further developed our idea. We headed to Factory Zero, a unique live-work facility for entrepreneurs who are creating new businesses. The resident entrepreneurs live upstairs and work downstairs; if you have a meeting, you have it in one of the downstairs workspaces or on the patio. We dove into phoning our respective networks, saying, "Hey, I'm working on a top-secret company. It's in this genre, and it's with this individual. Will you advise? Will you this? Will you that? Will you get prepared and know that I'm going to ask more of you? I'll share more about what's going on in thirty or sixty days." It was an absolutely amazing day. It was a lot like those "start-up" weekends that they hold in the technology world when a few hundred aspiring entrepreneurs have forty-eight hours to meet a co-founder and present their business concepts—the best company wins. We did everything that those entrepreneurs did in forty-eight hours, but we did it in one day with only two people. And it was the most efficient, productive, exhilarating, exciting, fun day I've ever had in my life.

After a few hours, we decided to leave because Ido had made a promise to his family that he'd be home by 5 p.m. every day that he was in town. Before we left, Ido asked me, "So, are you excited? What are you thinking about all this?"

I replied, "I'm excited, yes. If I seem like I'm not that excited, one thing you need to know about me is that I'm big on planning, and I'm big on details. I'm super excited, but my mind is racing."

Ido asked, "So where is your mind racing to?"

I said, "My mind is going exactly here: company name, trademark, operations, legal stuff, incorporation, up and running, picking a PR firm, branding around the name, branding everything else—from logo to website to the look—and making sure we can get the URL. I'm thinking about hiring the first two or three core people, along with the right interns, if need be. Yes, I'm super excited but my head is in all these places." He looked at me and put his right hand up. I put my right hand up, and we gave each other a high five.

Ido and his wife, Ronit, invited me to dinner that evening, and I was able to meet his children, who are within six months and a year, respectively, of my own. It was a great opportunity to get to know the man I was going into business with on an entirely different level.

Later that evening, there was a charity event for an organization called the Mama Hope Foundation, founded by our mutual friend Nyla Rodgers, who we knew through Summit Series, a highly private invitation-only group of leaders that meet at an annual conference and work to inspire and connect entrepreneurs, artists, musicians, and nonprofit leaders. Ido planned to attend, so I went with him. We ran into a bunch of people at the event that we both knew; it was a confirmation that this new business was a good move for us and that we were going in the right direction. As we got out of the car, I said to Ido, "Look, we're probably going to run into a lot of people we know—what do you want to say when someone asks us what we're up to? Should we tell them we're working on a 'stealth start-up,' like everyone else in San Francisco?"

But Ido had a different idea. He said, "Let's call it our 'top-secret project' and let everybody know that we're going into business together."

So that's what we did, and everyone was buzzing—wondering what we were up to. "Oh my God, Lauren Maillian and Ido Leffler doing something together? So what is it?" "Is it organic?" "Is it natural?" "Is it clothing? It must be fashion—or beauty."

Of course, Ido and I were smirking, "We can't tell you; it's top secret!" But it was an absolute confirmation that this was going to be an amazing opportunity, a great partnership, and that this awesome future lay ahead of us.

For me, this was a major claim-it-and-shine moment (see Chapter 8 for more on the concept of "claim it and shine"). Together, Ido and I had sketched out the beginnings of an ambitious brand that had game-changing potential for the beauty industry while making a meaningful impact by giving back. We're in a socially conscious society today, where people want to know that they're doing good—even with the products and purchases that they make. It's the new way of making philanthropy accessible. We ultimately said, "Let's focus on getting the company right, and let's come up with one nonprofit that is most deserving and really fits our mission best and who we believe in and have a connection with."

My experience in media has been a long time in the making, rooted in a deep passion for storytelling and public engagement. I co-hosted Oxygen's *Quit Your Day Job*, a platform that allowed me to connect with and mentor aspiring entrepreneurs. This rich experience was complemented by my involvement hosting CNBC's one-hour special, *The Unstoppables*, and my role as the first Lifestyle Expert on the *Tamron Hall Show*.

Each of these roles provided unique opportunities to expand my network, skills, and refine my connections. *Quit Your Day Job* not only allowed me to guide entrepreneurs but also enabled me to build relationships with industry experts, investors, and fellow mentors. Being part of *The Unstoppables* and the *Tamron Hall Show* further broadened my reach, connecting me with influential figures in the media industry and beyond. I've learned how to mentor on TV, host informative business interviews, share life stories, and even learned how to sell products online during the time when content-to-commerce was becoming the moneymaking media boom.

LESSONS IN NETWORKING

Every person you meet can offer a new perspective or opportunity, so it's important to treat each connection with respect and genuine interest. Your network should be dynamic, continuously assessed, and cultivated to ensure mutual benefits. Under the tutelage of Candi Carter, Oprah's former executive producer of over fifteen years, I honed my skills as a media personality. These lessons in maximizing on-camera time, delivering compelling messages, and becoming a brand steward were invaluable. They prepared me to diversify my media presence further, opening doors to more speaking opportunities and setting the stage for upcoming projects.

Candi Carter's mentorship was a pivotal moment in my career. Her guidance not only enhanced my media skills but also expanded my understanding of audience engagement. Through her, I learned the importance of leveraging every one of my life experiences to build and strengthen connections with my audience. This was a skill she had honed while working with Oprah as her executive producer, teaching how to use personal experiences to create a deep, personal connection with viewers.

Candi taught me how to make people feel like they know me through a TV screen, to feel comfortable with me, and to trust my recommendations. This ability to connect with an audience is crucial in building a network effect and Candi introduced me to a broader ability to use my gift to build bigger network effects. This is similar to the "Oprah effect," where people feel a personal connection with someone they have never met but consistently tune in to listen to and watch them.

Additionally, Candi taught me how to sell on camera, a skill that was deeply uncomfortable for me before. I never felt at ease using my presence to come on video and sell something, especially my own products. When I launched my personal branding boot camp, it was uncomfortable to ask for money directly; I really just wanted to help and transform people into their best selves. However, Candi showed me how to effectively sell through storytelling, perfecting what is now known as content-to-commerce.

This skill is invaluable in my executive media roles, where creating video content that drives commercial opportunities and sales is crucial. Candi's teachings helped me master selling in short sound bites, whether it was for a fifteen-second interstitial or a ninety-second segment. Her expertise was evident when she worked with Oprah, where one appearance could lead to products selling out instantly.

Mentors provide more than just knowledge; they can introduce you to this broader network effect. They teach you how to create a following of people who feel connected to you, want to listen to you, and trust your recommendations. This skill has been invaluable in my career, allowing me to build a loyal and engaged audience. In the world of media, this kind of connection is powerful, as it transforms viewers into dedicated supporters who feel personally invested in your journey.

PRACTICAL STEPS AND PERSONAL GROWTH

Each role you take on offers new networking opportunities. Embrace them fully and use them to expand your professional circle. Neglecting the ongoing cultivation of your network can limit your growth and opportunities. Regularly reach out to your connections, update them on your progress, and find ways to offer value to them. This keeps relationships active and beneficial.

Expanding your network requires intentional effort and a strategic approach. Attend industry events like conferences, seminars, and workshops to meet like-minded professionals. Engage actively, participate in discussions, and follow up with new contacts. Leverage social media platforms like LinkedIn and Twitter (now X) to share your insights, engage with others' content, and connect with professionals in your field. Joining professional organizations can provide access to exclusive networking events and resources. Remember, networking is a two-way street. Look for ways to help your connections, whether through introductions, sharing knowledge, or offering support.

Each new connection can teach you something valuable. Be open to learning and growing from these interactions. Strong relationships are built on trust, so be genuine, reliable, and supportive in your interactions. As you consider the people in your network, make no small plans. When you think big, you honestly never know where your connections will lead you. Be prepared for and open to anything.

My journey through various media roles has been as much about expanding my network as it has been about personal and professional growth. Each experience, from co-hosting *Quit Your Day Job* to my mentorship with Candi Carter, has provided invaluable lessons and connections that have shaped my career. For up-and-coming brand-builders and entrepreneurs, understanding the power of a strong and dynamic network is crucial. It's not just about who you know, but how you engage and grow with them that makes all the difference.

Building and refining a robust network is essential for personal and professional success. Embrace every opportunity to connect, learn, and offer value, and your network will become one of your greatest assets in achieving your goals.

Be a powerful venture magnet, attracting amazing opportunities into your life and business.

FOR REFLECTION

— **You don't have to be big to think and believe big.** Start getting comfortable with the latter. Believing in your potential and envisioning grand possibilities for yourself is the first step toward achieving greatness. No matter your current status or size, cultivating a mindset that embraces big dreams can set the stage for remarkable success. Reflect on how you can shift your thinking to embrace bold and ambitious goals.

— **Want more for yourself (theoretically) than anyone else ever could.** Your aspirations and dreams should be limitless. Often, others might set expectations for you, but it's essential to have an internal drive that surpasses any external benchmarks. Reflect on your deepest desires and ambitions and consider how you can nurture an insatiable drive to achieve more than anyone else might envision for you.

9

Take Control of Your own Voice

(Own Your Destiny)

I TOO HAVE HAD MY WINGS clipped. I have been be-littled. I had, at one time, my voice suppressed. And for years, I practiced a very important skill: taking control of my own voice.

I often wonder who I could have become without the financial and emotional strain of my divorce. How many companies could I have started or invested in? These thoughts sometimes make me sad or aggravated, but I try to channel my energy into what I can achieve now.

At twenty-four, with two kids, including a newborn, I was incredibly naive. I had placed so much trust, faith, and identity into being a wife, perhaps even more than being a mother. I was proud and excited to be young and married, fulfilling the expectation to take pride in my role as a wife, which hampered my independence.

One thing my ex-husband said to me, something I will never forget, was when he looked at me and made it clear that he would never financially support me or the children, telling me not to bite the hand that feeds me. That moment stuck with me because it was the day I decided I would do whatever it took to change my life and make money for myself and my kids.

Enduring various forms of abuse in my first marriage took a toll on my confidence, affecting how I showed up in the world. I'll never forget when my friends came over after he left to help me clean out his stuff from the closet. They laughed at the kitten heels I owned—tiny, half-inch or one-inch high—because he was just about an inch taller than me. I wore those heels to avoid being taller than him, which seemed acceptable when I was younger, thinking it was honoring his wishes. But I now recognize it as controlling behavior that stifled my self-expression, confidence, and independence.

When I represented myself in court during the divorce, I was a pro se litigant, writing my own divorce papers, motions, and affidavits, asking the court for relief. I had no idea what I was doing but had to figure it out. A friend gave me the CPLR law book for New York, and I researched everything I could to defend myself and my kids, even though he showed up with multiple lawyers. That experience taught me resourcefulness and gave me my voice because I had no other option.

After years in Family Court, I've realized that fighting for the money I was owed took a toll on my career and mental health. I kept filing papers to maintain the court's automatic processes, but it drained my energy and resources. Shifting my focus from this fight allowed me to dedicate myself to my career, significantly impacting my success and opportunities.

Despite the hardships, these experiences shaped me into a fighter and a resilient woman. They taught me to take control of my voice, advocate for myself and my children, and ultimately led me to the successes I've achieved.

It's far too easy to lose your voice when you're living in the shadow of someone else or the name of your behemoth Fortune 500 company. And it's even more frustrating when your hard-earned recognition and accomplishments are lost in the shadow of your business partner or colleague. No one knows what you've accomplished if you don't own it in some way. Don't shy away from taking credit when credit is due. Own your contributions, own your voice, and own your success. Otherwise you're promoting your erasure.

I've worked really hard on owning my voice and it's so important for you—man or woman, young or old, accomplished or not—to do, too. We were put on this earth to own our voice, to own how people perceive us, and to own the track records that we develop for ourselves, no matter how many stops and starts there may be along the way. And while even today I take on more than I should at times, I never say "yes" to anything that I don't have a genuine interest in or a project that I won't be able to be "all in" on.

Taking control of your own voice—like taking control of your own destiny—can be a remarkably powerful and liberating feeling, one that will impact how you live the rest of your life. After I decided to sell my interest in the winery, I knew that I wanted to firmly stake my personal values and reputation on my future ideas, endeavors, and new opportunities.

MAILLIAN

WHAT I'VE LEARNED ABOUT BUSINESS FROM MY COLLEAGUES

M ake knowledge of self a priority. Most people don't understand themselves well enough to effectively strategize their own success. Self-knowledge frees us up to know other people and the world in a more intelligent and meaningful way.

Do the thing and you will have the power. A lot of people expend massive amounts of energy avoiding the actual work they need to do to be successful. It's easy to get caught up in networking, reading, thinking, and planning, but ultimately, it's the work that will earn the accolades and the work that leads to new opportunities.

Creating and honoring my vision independent of other people's opinions has been pivotal for me. Most people assume that when they don't understand something, it doesn't make sense. This is false; true innovators have to bear being misunderstood while they build something new. I have been in multiple seasons of my life where people on the outside didn't understand me or my choices. Later, those same people hailed me as brilliant or insightful for those same choices. Everybody "gets" genius after it's obvious. Like Michelangelo sculpting David, we have to keep creating what's in our mind's eye and let everyone else catch on later.

—LISA NICOLE BELL, *CEO, Inspired Life Media Group*

I wanted to do something far more scalable and creative, and I wanted my own personal brand to be both easy to remember and transferable to any one of the ventures I was considering doing next—so much so that my next business was dubbed LMB, for Luxury Market Branding, now Leverage Momentum Build. It certainly didn't hurt that this acronym for my new business was the same as my initials at that time. This made for easy online searchability!

MAILLIAN: FINDING YOUR VOICE

People bet on the jockey, not the horse. You own your reputation and it often determines how far and where you go.

I honestly believe that you have to figure out a way to create some sort of subject matter expertise, thought leadership, or authority on an issue to be relevant and to get noticed and stay in the game. Writing and developing my own voice as an entrepreneur helped me get back in the game by creating thought leadership in those areas I knew best, and it allowed me to express who I truly am and my unique viewpoints. If I'd had a personal blog I would have been blogging, but I didn't, so I knew the best way to do it was to align myself with companies and organizations that gave me a voice, where I had something to say that mattered to them.

I began writing for several well-known media outlets that align with my brand, including *Forbes* and *Fast Company*, and created a fairly active social media presence. Through writing, I was able to publicly embrace my voice: I am an entrepreneur and I want to share (and own) my own experience and advice. I've kind of avoided being labeled as an entrepreneur for many years, and I avoided joining organizations for entrepreneurs, of which there are many. I didn't want to be part of some rah-rah club that would divert my energies from actually doing what I do best, which is working—and working hard.

I stayed firm in that belief until I realized that there might be some value to me in joining some of these entrepreneurship organizations. By joining a couple of these organizations, my eyes, my world, and my network were opened to a community I never knew existed. Before I joined, all my friends were significantly older than I was, and they still are. But when I joined a couple of these entrepreneur organizations, I quickly realized there are other really young, smart, driven but mature people like me who are also running companies and who aren't still trying to figure out what they are going to be when they grow up. Many of the people I met in these organizations were extremely driven, and they had the same special qualities that I had, which is why they were running successful businesses. These organizations connected me with people who share my values, vision, and voice, leading to tremendous growth in my life and business.

If you're an entrepreneur and you've been hanging back from participating in an entrepreneur organization, I suggest that you find one that's active in your community and that you start attending meetings. I think you'll be surprised by how valuable it can be to get together with a group of like-minded business people, and how many opportunities will come your way as a result.

Lauren Maillian

WHAT I'VE LEARNED ABOUT BUSINESS FROM MY COLLEAGUES

1. Get comfortable with being uncomfortable: Always be reaching way outside your comfort zone—that is where great change and growth happen.

2. Build and nurture your relationships: Know who you know and who they know. Spend time. Give. Especially before making an ask—but don't be afraid to make it!

3. Have a big, crazy, audacious vision for yourself and act on it.

I've taken big, crazy leaps into opportunities with steep learning curves, which was both exhilarating and stomach-churning, and each and every time, the opportunity came through a friend, former colleague, or acquaintance. Relationships really, really matter.

—KATHLEEN WARNER, *Senior Advisor, America Achieves*

Your personal reputation drives your ability to enter the networks you want to get into to achieve your goals, and this reputation is often connected to your job. Your network is the new currency of success. You have to know not only how to build and create your networks but also how to work within them.

The quality of your networks is connected to your success and the reputation that you have within those networks is connected to your job. Every move you make is monitored in some way. You may not necessarily notice who's monitoring you at any given time—it may be something that's uncovered days, weeks, or even years later.

I mostly agree with Kathleen's thoughts above, but I also think that you can focus your efforts on your personal productivity, while being confident enough to push yourself to engage in opportunities that force you beyond your comfort zone and make you stronger. This means you need to learn to maximize your personal productivity by focusing on doing what you do best and delegating the rest. I have found that I'm a much better version of me when I delegate the routine tasks to someone else and spend the majority of my time doing what I do best. I'm more productive, effective, and happier.

Return every call and email; you never know who's behind the message or where the communication could lead. What you put out comes back and life has a funny way of putting people in unexpected places and positions. Know who you are and what you stand for and what you want to be. Be able to clearly communicate it and also be consistent across all your platforms about how you're communicating who you are and what you're about. Place relationships at the top of your list of priorities.

Relationships are the currency of influence and success in business. No matter how badly you want to get ahead, never ever step on someone to do it. Remember: You never know who's watching. Become skilled at working within your network. Learn how to evaluate when and how to share the connections in your network with other people. Know when it's appropriate to open and share your network with outsiders.

Anyone you introduce to your network is a reflection of you. Think about the time constraints and responsibilities for those in your network, and don't dilute your clout with your own connections by making tons of blind, misguided, or ill-informed introductions. When in doubt, don't do it. I can't stand it when someone makes a judgment about what they think my business skills or experience are by looking at me and not getting to know who I really am.

I think it's easy for people to try to pigeonhole you: You're young, you're old, you're a woman, you're a man, you're an experienced business person who brings a lot to the table—or you're not. Whenever someone tries to stick a label on me before they take the time to figure out who I really am, or to do the research before they meet me, I make a point to correct the situation immediately. Yes, I'm a woman, and, yes, I'm in my thirties, but I've built three successful ventures—and I'm in the process of building more—and I serve on a number of boards and I mentor up-and-coming entrepreneurs. Anything that people could undervalue me for or expect me to have that I don't have or could expect me to do that I don't do, I say, "That's not me." When I meet someone new, I don't allow them to make assumptions about me.

Although you can't control other people's opinions of you, there's value in being able to control your own voice. Opinions will come and go—both negative and positive at times—but you hold the power to continue to be deliberate in your communication and firm in your way.

FOR REFLECTION

- Be consistent in your external communications, whether it's email messages, checking in with a colleague, a newsletter, or social media posting.

- Take control of your own voice.

- Find ways to create thought leadership in your areas of expertise.

- Research which organizations align with your goals and values and then join the ones that will help broaden or deepen your network.

- When joining these organizations, know how you can add value and quickly get to work.

- Find the like-minded people in your professional space and create a community that allows you to have a platform to share experiences.

- Realize the power of your silence and know when to hold still.

- Your network is the new currency of success. Master how to build a meaningful and genuine network and how to protect it from the noise and intrusions that will dilute your marginal value to the network.

- Treat everyone well. Make everyone feel big.

- You never know who's on the other end of a phone call.

5

Exceed Expectations

(Build a Legacy of Success)

HOW DO YOU MEASURE SUCCESS? To me, true success comes when you build a legacy of success. This happens when you are able to set a series of aspirational goals and then achieve them repeatedly throughout your life. Everyone goes through a journey on the path to a lifetime of success, but the measurable marks are different. Your success is made so that you can pass it down to others; that is, your own example of success can inspire others to set their own aspirational goals and then achieve them—creating their own legacies of success.

We can't close the success gap around women until we close the success-ambition gap. We need more women who strive to be ambitious, who wake up and say, "I really want to do well. I really want to succeed. I really want to be powerful. I really want to be in control."

We've got to have more women who really want these things in order to create a more balanced view of what success looks like.

I personally know I am successful when I attract opportunities. Opportunities come to me because I have established a reputation for being the kind of person who consistently exceeds expectations and delivers what is promised—and often much, much more. I work extremely hard, and I won't take on a project unless I'm willing to commit myself 110 percent. Case in point, my business partner Jeremy Johnson and I were scheduled to attend a potential investor meeting, but a half hour before start time, I received a text message from Jeremy that said, "Sorry. Emergency at the office. Can't make it."

My response was, "Okay, I got it," which meant, I can do this without you and the outcome will be as good if not better.

The people in my networks know that when they send an opportunity my way, they can rest assured that if I agree to take it on, I won't merely be in—I'll be all in. I don't make small plans. I get things done. I never make excuses. These are a few of my core values—they're why people are attracted to working with me. But these values aren't exclusive to me. If you exhibit the same values in your business life, you will attract the same kind of people and opportunities I do.

Make no mistake about it, success is no accident. Successful people might make it look easy, but from my own personal experience—and the experience of the successful people I've met and worked with—I have learned that it's not easy. Every person who has achieved great success in his or her life has overcome numerous challenges, and has faced failure, sometimes many times over. Every success I've experienced—as well as every failure—has helped to prepare me for even more success in the future. So far, I have had the good fortune to start up three very successful businesses: Sugarleaf Vineyards, Luxury Market Branding, and Gen Y Capital Partners. But while I have experienced a good run of success, like every other entrepreneur, I sometimes lie awake at night worrying about the possibility that one of my ventures will go off the rails. The uncertainty keeps me nimble, alert, and responsive! At times the unknown can be nerve-racking, but more often than not, it forces me to be hypersensitive to the multitude of circumstances that could adversely, or positively, affect my business interests. The pro to sleeping with one eye open, as they say, is that I never miss a beat!

EXCEED EXPECTATIONS

So, how can you improve the odds that you'll achieve the success you want in life? I asked one of my personal heroes, Mellody Hobson, what success means to her and what she thinks it was that enabled her to be so successful. Mellody has been president of the Chicago-based investment management firm Ariel Investments since 2000, and she serves on the board of directors of Starbucks, DreamWorks Animation, and Estée Lauder.

Mellody explained to me that success for her is a personal sense of accomplishment, and that it's something in her own head. She doesn't look for outside recognition or accolades. According to Mellody, she has never been nor ever will be motivated by other people. She told me that her perspective on success is best summed up in the classic Boy Scout motto, "Be prepared," and that she is always prepared. The only time her confidence lacks is when she is not as prepared as she would like to be.

When Mellody told me this, I realized that she was absolutely right. Being prepared for opportunities as they present themselves is a quality that's so simple yet so powerful, but it's often overlooked.

Many times people allow events to happen and then hope for the best—they don't bring their best selves to the table. As I thought about my own life, I realized that much of my success was a direct result of being prepared—I was ready for opportunity when it knocked on my door. Actually, I was more than ready for it—I invited it to come in, kick off its shoes, and join me for dinner.

As far as the actual reasons for her success, Mellody attributes it to outworking everyone else. She has an unwavering work ethic, original ideas, and she makes a point of always coming through. According to studies done at Ariel Investments, nearly 80 percent of people don't live up to their commitments. That's a terrible track record when you think about it, and it is an indication of how rare (and welcome) it is to work with someone who does consistently live up to his or her commitments. If you can be that person, you will stand head and shoulders above the rest of the pack, and believe me, you will be noticed. And you will exceed expectations.

I have many friends who are also successful entrepreneurs, and I now look at how they achieved their successes in a new way. Whereas, in the past, I may have assumed it was more organic—through much trial and error—I now realize that each one of them was as prepared as could possibly be for the opportunities that catapulted him or her forward. The combination of their experiences, successes, failures, networks, colleagues, and supporters—all these and more—put them in the right place at the right time to take advantage of a specific opportunity when it arrived.

The summer of 2013 was going to be devoted to writing the first edition of this book and spending time with my family. But when Ido Leffler invited me to San Francisco to explore a new joint business venture with him (see Chapter 3), I was prepared. Not only was I personally prepared, but I was prepared to prioritize my calendar to make it work. I intuitively knew that I absolutely had to embrace this opportunity, no matter what happened. The potential for building something very big that would have a positive impact on the lives of many people was as clear as day to me, and I was drawn to it. I was intrigued by the opportunity to broaden my knowledge base, deepen my relationships, and explore the opportunity. At the time, the experience in and of itself trumped the outcome!

It's funny how it worked out because I had purposefully designed my schedule to have a summer that was far less hectic than my usual pace so I could concentrate on writing this book and spending time with my children, who are growing up before my eyes. But when you're an entrepreneur, I have found that there's always room for more.

When I started LMB Group, creating this kind of business—a strategic brand-building and marketing consultancy serving the wine and spirits, beauty, and consumer products industries—wasn't necessarily at the forefront of my mind in terms of what was next for me, but I was prepared and well equipped to do it. I had the wherewithal, know-how, expertise, skills, and the network—along with the drive and the time I needed—plus I knew this kind of business inside out. It was where my network needed my involvement and where I could add the most incremental value at the time.

Today LMB Group has evolved into a global strategic advisory firm renowned for its expertise and influence. We partner with high-growth consumer brands and organizations to leverage momentum and build their strategic goals. We specialize in creating tailored blueprints that drive sustainable and scalable breakthroughs.

Lauren
MAILLIAN

WHAT I'VE LEARNED ABOUT BUSINESS FROM MY COLLEAGUES

C arola Jain, CEO and Co-Founder of DMINTI, is always planning ahead in her own mind so as never to be unprepared. She is elegant, poised, and globally aware in every facet of her life, which allows her to have a perspective on the world that transcends all industries, personalities, cultures, and socioeconomic statuses. It's undoubtedly why she has been so successful both professionally and personally. Here's her advice about business:

1. Never let anyone tell you that you can't do it!

2. Work hard and you will reap the benefits.

3. Never stop reading!

4. Traveling makes people more open-minded.

And when it came time for Gen Y Capital Partners, I was as prepared as I have ever been for anything. I had spent a year advising technology start-ups on marketing, branding, strategy, and business development. I understood marketing, consumer engagement, on-line-user experience, data analytics, and digital trends. But the start-ups taught me about the culture and fundamentals of technology, as well as the back end of the digital landscape and how much coding went into implementing my marketing plans. I quickly grew and learned where I needed to know more. My advisory role seemed in part mutual, and at times reciprocal, because we all learned and grew.

Investing in early-stage companies was something I had been deeply and actively involved in, and I was eager and excited to have the opportunity to learn more about it, to dive in even deeper. I was prepared for the opportunity when it arrived. I was also prepared to scale back from other activities in my business and personal life to give myself time to further explore this industry.

At the Metropolitan Museum of Art, I sit on the Multicultural Audience Development Initiative (MADI) advisory board that advises the museum's Department of External Affairs about ways to broaden support and attract attendance from all of New York's communities. There are a number of remarkable people on the board, including Emily Rafferty, the Met's president, and museum executives Harold Holzer and Donna Williams.

I am currently the youngest person on the Met's board. I believe the reason I was invited to join them is because I bring not only the same level of commitment to philanthropy as they do but also something unique: a youthful perspective. This is something that many established cultural institutions are looking for today—they are committed to attracting and engaging young people to maintain their relevance to society as a cultural institution. Multifaceted perspective is extremely important for a venerable institution like the Metropolitan Museum of Art.

The Met benefits from the perspective and contributions that I can provide to maintain connectivity to the youthful, vibrant, and hip culture of future generations. Regardless, the day I was inducted into that particular advisory board at the museum after a formal vote, all eyes were on me and I felt the distinct sense of the pressure of everyone's expectations of me and my future contributions. The bar was high, but it didn't scare me—it motivated me.

MAILLIAN: BUILDING A LEGACY OF SUCCESS

Building a legacy of success occurs when you are able to set a series of aspirational goals and then achieve them repeatedly throughout your lifetime.

The museum is at the forefront of the art world, yet that doesn't guarantee its connectivity with future generations of patrons. Every established institution—including the Met—can only do this if it has its fingers planted firmly on the pulse of what drives these young men and women and what will pique their interest. I know that I bring an important and unique perspective to the committee because I contribute meaningful insight, data, context, ideas, perspective, and ways to engage younger donors earlier in their philanthropic life cycle so that, as they become more mature and established, the museum is top of mind for serious charitable donations.

Participating on these kinds of boards is a great way to network with people who can help you attain your own goals in business and in life, whatever they may be. For example, sitting next to you in a nonprofit board meeting might be the president of a local bank, the founder of a highly successful business, and other movers and shakers in your community. By routinely exceeding the expectations of your fellow board members, you will definitely stick out—in a good way— and all kinds of opportunities may result. Remember: Successful people like to work and spend time with other successful people. If you shine, then others will be attracted to your light.

One of the activities I do to be prepared for opportunities when they arrive is to keep active in my networks. This means regularly picking up the phone and keeping in touch with and engaging with my network of business contacts before I need a favor, not when I all of a sudden need their help yesterday. I'm drawn to them and they're drawn to me. Keeping my network warm is a natural part of how I socialize. The kind of people I enjoy spending my time with are those people who are either like me—driven, resilient—or who complement me and my perspective, and who create balanced dialogue and interactions. My life is intentionally designed to maximize the personal time I spend with people who I admire and respect professionally.

They are integral parts of my ecosystem as I am of theirs.

Stay actively involved in your network and keep all of your connections warm at all times, even as you add new people to your network. If you don't know who your LinkedIn connections are, and if you haven't figured out what you've got in common or how you can help one another in some simple and direct ways, then you really aren't leveraging your network. You must be prepared to engage them and explore a possible business deal with them, or solicit their involvement or expertise.

The more diverse the network you build, the better the chance you'll get called to participate in something that will bring you closer to achieving your goals. The more exposure you have to people who offer these opportunities, the better because they'll think about you when something comes up. They'll go through that Rolodex in their heads and ask, "Now, who would be the right person for this position?" And all of a sudden they'll think of you—the committed, driven, smart person they met at breakfast whose expertise aligns with their organizational needs.

I've always worked hard to build and maintain a diverse group of friends, and a really diverse network of business contacts. This network includes people who inspire me to be the best mother, the best friend,

the best CEO, the best investor, advisor, entrepreneur, and philan-
thropist I can possibly be. I have found that I need various forms of
inspiration and stimulation to motivate me to be a better me in every
facet of my life and business. To build out a great team for your business
or company, you shouldn't have to look far outside your network if it
aligns with and complements your strengths, interests, and values.

David Jones, former Global Chief Executive Officer of Havas, is
the epitome of creating success on your own terms. He became the
youngest Global CEO in the history of advertising after he started a
career as an accountant and co-founded One Young World, a nonprofit global youth forum. David knows exactly what qualities most
often lead to success in business, so here are some of his thoughts on
the topic:

> The consistent factor that most successful people will play back
> when asked about their success is that they never gave up. You
> have to be relentless. Also, focus is key. Most smart people can
> spot an opportunity or problem. Most smart people can put in
> place the right strategy to capitalize on it. But the thing that
> separates those who succeed from those who fail is to ensure
> that 100 percent of their efforts are totally focused on what will
> lead to success and to not be distracted no matter how many
> other seemingly important things get in the way.

Finally, I think the expression "Success has many parents, failure
is an orphan" is actually true, but not in the way it's usually used. The
usual way is to imply everyone taking credit for a good idea, [but]
more in the sense that you will find it very hard to succeed alone.
Build a great team. Learn from and rely on other people. Share the
success (and the stress and worries!). Happy, talented teams win in
sport and in business.

I agree that "success has many parents." I believe that some of those "parents" are the people we look up to in life; they are people that inspire us to reach for the stars and to bring the best of what we have to offer to the table. In my case, and I would guess this is true of most people, I don't have only one person I look up to.

There are a variety of people who inspire me—some I know and some I don't. As for the latter, it's okay that I don't have access to and personal relationships with them because I'm most interested in monitoring how they handle adversity and success under pressure, and how they respond in the press. You can learn a lot by observing how they protect and communicate their personal brand and how they rebound under the weight of public opinion. It's fascinating—you should try it!

One woman that I most admire—particularly in the area of media and marketing—is Arianna Huffington. After more than a decade of standing in the shadow of her husband, former Congressman Michael Huffington, she divorced in 1997, found her own voice, and started The Huffington Post, which she sold to AOL in 2011 for $315 million. When I think about someone who has made his or her mark as a powerhouse in the marketing, advertising, and media world, I automatically think of Arianna Huffington.

According to Arianna, the secret to networking is focus and attention:

> The most important quality is attention—like are you really present, fully present? I think you can be fully present even at a cocktail party when you're standing and there's noise. Even if you have a two-minute conversation, if you are not looking over to see if there's somebody more interesting to talk to, or you're not preoccupied with something else—I know there's this incredibly overused and abused word, networking.[1]

When it comes to being a behind-the-scenes, influential, well-respected, incredibly brilliant businesswoman who commands the respect of those with whom she works, I think of someone like Loida Lewis, whose late husband, Reginald Lewis—founder of TLC Beatrice—was the first Black billionaire. Today, Loida is chairwoman of the company, and although she's likely to be one of the most petite women you've ever seen, she can walk into any room—from the Harvard Club, to a black-tie event, to the boardroom—and command the same level of respect that you would think only Fortune 500 company men get.

I also admire quite a few businessmen, especially those who believe in and take chances on unproven women who they suspect may have the potential to be the next CEO and who they trust will work hard to understand all the facets of what is going on so that they can bring a meaningful perspective to the table. Ultimately, these are the men who are confident enough in themselves and their own abilities to give the professional limelight to a woman who may very well steal the show!

One of the businessmen I most admire is Richard Edelman. Richard is chairman and CEO of Edelman, the largest public relations firm in the world. In addition to his sheer brilliance and PR talent, I admire Richard for his campaign to put women in senior executive positions within his 4,800-person-strong business. For much the same reasons, I also admire Facebook founder Mark Zuckerberg. Not only is he technically brilliant, but he has also made it a point to hire and promote women into key positions within the company—Sheryl Sandberg is just one of many. I am hopeful that other business leaders will follow the examples set by these two men.

Each of the people I look up to inspires me by their ability to do one thing particularly well. In fact, I don't know one person that I admire who I can look at and say that he or she does everything well. Instead, I look at each of the people I admire and extract the most information from that person's core competency.

- ► Think about the answers to these questions:
- ► How do you define success?
- ► What people inspire you?
- ► What are you doing today to find the success you hope to achieve in the future?

Ultimately, the answers to these questions are what define you. What's most important to keep in mind when you're thinking about how you define success is that you need to find success in a way that you are comfortable with, not what your business partner is comfortable with, or your spouse, or your mentor, etc. This is really important to remember. Only you have to walk in your shoes, and only you have to be proud of your journey. I don't try to live up to anyone else's standards except for my own. Admittedly, I set very high standards for myself, but that's my decision, and it only has to work for me and no one else.

A colleague of mine, Adelaide Lancaster, cowrote a book titled *The Big Enough Company: Creating a Business That Works for You* (Portfolio Hardcover, 2011) that touches on this very topic. The book suggests that readers ask themselves, "How big is big enough for me?" Not everyone needs or wants to start a company that is going to grow like mad. *To you* is directly related to how you define success for yourself in business and in life.

Build something greater than yourself—something that builds a legacy and inspires and encourages others to do something great because your life is also about the effect you have on other people's lives. It's about the perspective that you bring to the table.

Be more interested than interesting, especially when you're new to the game. Show that you're committed, dedicated, inquisitive, and working hard to understand all the facets and perspectives of what's going on. Soak up as much knowledge as you can so that you can be an informed speaker.

Frame your work and your story and messaging in terms of where you want to be and who you want to be in the future, not necessarily on where and who you are today. Make big plans. If you want the option of staying in, then start out aiming high. Just never step on someone to get ahead. As long as it is moral and ethical, is not at the detriment of someone or something else, and does not compromise yourself or your integrity, you should define success in a way that works best for you and what you ultimately want out of life.

Once you define what successful would look like for you, the next step is to map out a plan that's going to get you there. Remember: this plan has to work for you only and for no one else. (See Chapter 3 for details about how to set goals and make plans for your success.)

If your definition of success means putting your children in private school and living in a big apartment in the city, with a nice summer home on the beach, that's fine—if that's what makes you feel most comfortable, then that's exactly what you should plan for. And if you want all the bling to go along with your success—the big diamonds, huge wardrobes full of designer couture, Bentley in the driveway— and you want to flaunt it for all to see, that's okay, too. You've got the right to define success in your own terms and to display it however you like. Success for me, however, means something different.

It's the ability to do what I love professionally, on my own terms, in a way that aligns with my social mission, while also being financially rewarding and profitable. My goals are to live life comfortably, raise my children well, and have enough capacity to give back in a meaningful way to those who are less fortunate—all while feeling good about the decisions I have made along the way. I have met and spent time with some of the most successful men and women on this planet, and I have found that many of these truly successful people are also some of the most humble individuals you could ever imagine meeting. They don't have to show off their wealth or live ostentatiously to feel successful and good about themselves. In my experience, the most successful people are hungrier for success than they are for attention.

But remember: Success is whatever you want it to be, so make sure that you're working to fulfill your own dreams and nobody else's. The only reward that really counts is the one that causes you to say to yourself, "I did it. I achieved exactly what I hoped and dreamed I would achieve." If you're constantly asking, "What do my peers think of me?" or "How will this success affect how people look at me?" then I don't think you're on the right track for success in your life. That kind of motivation isn't going to provide you with the extremely high levels of energy and purpose that you'll need over a sustained period of time to turn your business dreams into reality. A meteoric rise is exciting, but sustained success is far more valuable and rewarding. Though it can be tempting at times, don't lose sight of what's genuinely important to you: furthering your dreams and defining success in a way that works for you.

Of course, even the most successful people never truly arrive at their ultimate destinations—in my experience, they are always striving to be the best men or women they can be. But everyone reaches milestones in their lives—a promotion gained, a child born, a business taken public through a successful IPO—and these are the times when you can step back for a moment and give yourself a pat on the back for doing the actions you said you would, committing to the actions you committed to, and achieving the goals that you wanted to achieve.

Treat your business life as if it is a perpetual interview. Someone is always watching your every move and analyzing your decisions—make sure it works for you and not against you. You want to be in the position where someone comes up to you some day and says, "I've been following your career and professional trajectory for years, and I know you have what it takes for this next opportunity," instead of someone saying behind your back, "Nope, I've watched him burn bridges, make irrational decisions, and talk poorly about his colleagues for the past five years. That's not the kind of person I want to work with."

Interactions you have with a client, colleague, or friend today may be the unofficial interview for your dream job in three years, or your experiences with them may keep you top of mind for something a colleague of theirs is hiring for. You never know what opportunities are waiting for you down the road. But what you can control is your reputation, and you do that every day with your actions.

Finally, I believe that success is meaningless if you can't enjoy it with your family and those who matter most to you. Of course, you will have to decide for yourself who—or what—is most important to you. And once you've decided, then go after it—with everything you've got.

FOR REFLECTION

- Be a person of your word. So few people are.

- Show that you are committed to following through.

- Get used to proving yourself even after you feel you're accomplished in some right. Ordinary people get comfortable; extraordinary people always want to do and be better.

- Do what needs to be done without explicit direction. Show that you are capable of taking the reins.

- Never get too comfortable with where you are. Someone always wants your place, and they're patiently waiting for you to slip.

- Never lose sight of what matters most in your life—your success is empty without those you love.

6

Reinvent Yourself

(And Your Business)

W HEN IT COMES TO FRIENDS, lovers, and businesses, it's easy to let emotions get in the way of rational decision-making. Leaving behind my winery and starting something new—(LMB)—was not easy for me to do. Although I was hungry for new opportunities and challenges, so much of who I was and how others perceived me had become wrapped up with the winery. I had become Lauren, the Young and Successful Winery Owner, and I was very emotionally invested in that role—so much so that I dreamed each of my children would have the opportunity to be married there one day.

However, I eventually realized that the winery was just the first stop on my entrepreneurial journey and that I would have to reinvent myself if I hoped to make it to the next destination. While some entrepreneurs (I call them builders) stay with the business they founded as long as they possibly can—sometimes retiring after decades of building and operating their businesses and sometimes being forced out by a board of directors looking for younger blood— others (the initiators) get bored after getting their businesses up and running. They're constantly looking to take on the next challenge and create the next success. Reinventing yourself not only has the potential to put you on a new entrepreneurial path, but it can also open you up to entirely new networks of business and personal contacts.

As an entrepreneur, it's important for you to figure out if you're a builder or an initiator, because if you wind up in the wrong role, not only will you be unsatisfied with your situation, but you also won't give 110 percent of yourself 100 percent of the time. As you've probably guessed by now, I'm an initiator. I'm always looking for the next challenge, the next success.

My second business, LMB Group, was a direct result of pushing myself to think differently about who I was and who I had become to my family, friends, and business colleagues. It came from thinking, *Okay, I've run this winery for nearly eight years, and it's what my entire adult professional reputation has been founded on, but I've done everything I can do with the business. It's time for new challenges.* I was ready to reinvent myself—to move on from my persona of Lauren the Young and Successful Winery Owner to someone new. But I didn't know who that someone was yet.

To help figure that out, I focused on what I enjoyed most about operating the winery and what my greatest accomplishments had been. At the same time, I was trying to get a handle on what I wanted to do next in my entrepreneurial life—hopefully, something I would enjoy and excel at.

When I began the winery, I had very little knowledge about the industry, but I was an inquisitive sponge—hungry to learn everything there was to know about building a successful business. I sought out and tapped into the knowledge of some of the most experienced, successful, and well-respected people in the industry, and I was never shy about asking questions—and listening to the advice I obtained. I didn't always put the advice I received into practice in my own business, but I definitely considered it, and I was grateful to have it.

Wineries are among the most highly regulated businesses in our country, and compliance with all the different federal, state, and local laws and regulations is a huge headache for business owners, but it was something I actually enjoyed and was good at.

Because of this, I considered starting a company that would take care of the back-end compliance issues for other wineries. We would charge a premium to handle all the mundane and annoying administrative tasks that every winery owner has to deal with. I figured it would be easy to sign up a bunch of clients for a business like that, which would allow winery owners to focus on making great wine and growing their businesses instead of dealing with all the time-consuming government-required paperwork and red tape.

WHAT I'VE LEARNED ABOUT BUSINESS FROM MY COLLEAGUES

Kelly Hoey, author of *Build Your Dream Network*, attained her success early on in the more traditional route as an attorney. I admire how she has redirected the skills that made her a successful attorney and created success around her interests in technology and start-ups on her own terms. Here's her advice about business:

1. Follow your passion.

2. Focus on doing whatever you choose to do well.

3. With passion and excellence in execution, there will be success.

4. Confidence has had the greatest impact on my own success—and not being fearless but proceeding ahead in spite of my fears.

I quickly talked myself out of that idea, however, after I experienced my own nightmare of mounting paperwork and dreadful compliance issues with my own winery. I dealt with it, but I realized that the last thing I wanted to do was to fix these problems over and over again for someone else's business!

So, although I was great at the compliance end of the business, I knew I was also good at the marketing and branding of our products, building brand loyalty, and driving retail, wholesale, and online sales. Not only that, but I seemed to have a real knack for building partnerships that drove revenue, such as those with the media and tourism agencies, and engaging our consumers with our brand and driving sales to our online store.

So, I had to step back and consider what that would look like and what I would do. With the help of one of my trusted friends, it became clear that branding and marketing were what my business network needed most. These were also the two core areas where my expertise could have the most meaningful and measurable impact. It was also evident that people don't often have the opportunity to make money in the wine business, so there was a market ripe for someone to come in and help breathe life into wine companies that had grown complacent over the years or that needed an injection of youth and excitement. With that realization in hand, I started LMB.

My first client was Heritage Link Brands in Los Angeles, founded by Selena Cuffe. The company specializes in finding great African wines and importing and promoting them within the United States. I had met Selena four years earlier at one of my speaking engage-ments while she was an MBA student at Harvard (another example of networking turning an acquaintance into an opportunity). My first project with Heritage Link was helping the company rebrand and market a very special line of South African wines. These wines had done very well in South Africa and had deep roots there, but our goal was to make them just as successful here in the United States.

So, I went to South Africa with Selena and her team and helped them conduct tasting trials of the wines they wanted to bring into the United States. I provided advice on how to best refine the wines for the market given the desired price points, and we discussed rebranding and packaging. We conducted focus groups, and I met with the brand's founders to define the non-negotiable values of their family name and history—what they did and did not want to be shared in the media.

We talked about when and how we would ship the product to the United States and developed a distribution strategy. We had to consider which airlines we wanted to carry it, whether it would be available on domestic or international flights, how the product would be packaged, and whether or not we should offer it for presale.

Heritage Link wanted to introduce a young, fresh, and approachable brand to the U.S. market, and I advised them on how to establish brand equity and awareness. We worked extensively on how we would accomplish these goals—from the advertising tagline to the story we told, to the communication of how and why the family that owned the brand was involved, and how we would convey our mission across various media. The launch was a great success, and we met—and in some cases, exceeded—every one of the goals we set for its rollout. While I was still involved with wine, I was no longer involved in making it. Instead, I was successfully branding and marketing it.

I quickly realized that if I could do this successfully with wine, there was no reason I couldn't apply the same knowledge and expertise to other products and businesses. As I threw myself into my new business, LMB took on a variety of established and burgeoning brands as clients, quickly proving what we could do as a boutique firm that blended creative marketing insights with business development and partnerships.

Lauren

MAILLIAN: REINVENTING YOURSELF

I don't look like what I've been through. It's far easier to waste time entertaining and playing a part to fool your friends, but it's far more rewarding to innovate and emerge on higher ground.

Not only had I reinvented my business, but I had also reinvented myself and my relationships—something I would do again and again in the years to come. I am often asked about my own path in business: "How did you go from being a winery owner to a marketer, and then from being a marketer to a venture capitalist?" My answer is actually quite simple: "I did it by innovating as an entrepreneur. It has been the evolution of me and my interests."

Our generation isn't married to the past—we're not stuck doing whatever that major is on our college degree, and we're not frozen by the fear that a potential employer will view our eclectic and ever-changing resumes as an indicator of some sort of character or motivational defect. Smart businesspeople know that someone's skills and ability to look beyond conventional wisdom and innovate are far more important than any degree, title, or fancy business card.

So, the most important question for someone who wants to be successful today—and far into the future—is this: How do you evolve? More specifically, how do you explore your passions and creativity, and how do you figure out ways to continually develop or reinvent yourself and your businesses—both in a creative way and with a creative edge?

Whatever evolution you make in business has to be creative in order to be interesting and catch people's attention, whether you're working as an entrepreneur or in a corporate setting. The largest Fortune 500 companies today are including words like "creative," "innovative," and "entrepreneurial" in their position descriptions and job postings. For these large companies, this is something new. In the past, corporations valued and rewarded people who conformed to their company cultures and stayed within the strict boundaries that the companies defined for them. That's no longer the case—they now want people who think like entrepreneurs, who are intrapreneurial.

To me, versatility means that you do the following:

▶ **Leave your job description and comfort zone.** Do whatever is needed to maximize value creation. The more you step outside your comfort zone, the more value you can potentially create. You can do this either by realizing (1) a new passion or (2) new capabilities. I have learned that when you're an entrepreneur, you don't get the option to say, "Well, that's not my job." No—everything is your job, at least in the very beginning. If there's nobody else to do it, then there goes your company.

▶ **Be reliable.** You will build trust and goodwill by doing what you say you are going to do—when you say you are going to do it. Reliability helps you create a firm foundation from which you can quickly pivot when necessary as conditions demand it.

▶ **Be straightforward.** Most people in business prefer their business partners and colleagues to be honest and candid with them and not to beat around the bush. Being straightforward enables you to get to the heart of issues quickly and makes solving them much more efficient.

▶ **Show that you're self-motivated and naturally curious** and that you don't need to be motivated externally to learn or assist in solving problems. Companies put a premium on people who are self-motivated, who will pick up the slack and treat a company like their own, and who will solve problems that they're not asked specifically to solve. They are willing to

pay a premium for people who are naturally curious and motivated to effectuate change or get a project right. Be highly
motivated, skilled, and engaged. It takes these kinds of people
to make a business successful, no matter how big or small
it may be. You can work for Colgate-Palmolive, and when
you walk into a meeting, you're still John Doe who works
for Colgate-Palmolive. However, when you leave, people may
remember Colgate-Palmolive, but they're really going to
remember how John Doe conducted himself or herself—that's
where the greatest impression will be left. Your representation
as an employee of a company is your placeholder, but you're
always representing yourself, whether you're an employee or
an entrepreneur.

▶ **Show that you can identify weaknesses and create solutions.**
Every company wants a doer or a creator. Know your value-add
and get to work. One characteristic that's made me successful
is that I clearly say when I'm not good at something, if it's not
my area of expertise, or if my time is better spent being productive on another task. I am the first one to raise my hand
and say, "This is not my area of expertise." And rather than
being penalized for my inadequacies, I am respected for telling
people where my strengths are and ensuring that they are being
leveraged to the greatest degree possible.

▶ **Be a good and clear communicator.** Quality communica-
tors are transparent yet tactful, eloquent, and non-conde-
scending. This aligns with my belief that success stems from
being assertive and deliberate but not aggressive or abrasive.
It's essential to communicate your strategic intentions to

people in your network who can open doors or who are close to opportunities you'd like to be considered for. Note: This isn't about begging for work or appearing desperate; it's about putting out feelers in your network. A warm introduction is far better than a cold call when you have your sights set on a business opportunity. Moreover, if you apply for a job where a friend or colleague works and is highly regarded, but you haven't enlisted their assistance beforehand, it speaks volumes about how you explore and leverage opportunities as a businessperson—so don't let pride get in the way.

What does versatility mean to you? How can you be the kind of person who thinks like an entrepreneur, even if you're in the heart of a conservative, one-hundred-year-old multinational corporation?

All of these intrapreneurial skills are transferable to any position in any company—from start-up to the Fortune 500. Almost every company today seems to want people who are entrepreneurial in their thoughts and actions. Employers seek individuals who will step up and make things happen—not sit back and wait for things to happen to them. As management consultant Chris Smith wrote in a Harvard Business Review Blog Network post, these are the people who exude entrepreneurial spirit—the ones who want to learn, experiment, apply, share, and partner.[2]

In an article for *Fast Company* magazine, I listed five actions that entrepreneurs should consider before they reinvent themselves. With a little bit of tweaking, these tips are just as applicable for someone working within a large corporation as they are for a start-up entrepreneur. Be sure to consider these actions before you reinvent yourself, no matter what your job is or what company you work for.

► **Build a comprehensive support system.** Surround yourself with a support system of peer mentors who understand you, your business, and where you are in life. Develop and maintain relationships with successful, high-level, proven businesspeople that you respect, admire, and aspire to be like professionally to help you navigate and execute your plan. Bring on a trusted personal advisor to be a sounding board. Hire a business coach or a life coach if necessary.

► **Evaluate your strengths and skills.** Start by listing the business skills you used in your last position and the successes you achieved. Determine if your experience at your most recent company provided hands-on education that can help you launch your next venture. Many of your skills should carry over to your new venture, so identify any additional professional areas of expertise that may be needed and seek advice where necessary.

► **List your priorities.** Be clear about what's important to you and what you value most. Ensure that you can achieve your goals and objectives while maintaining a work-life balance throughout your transition. (More about the myth and reality of work-life balance in Chapter 7.) Your business should work for you, not against the equilibrium you create to make the transition manageable.

► **Clarify your vision.** Develop a mission statement for your business. Understand your market's demographics and how you will reach them. Immerse yourself in the industry you're targeting—absorb as much knowledge as possible and build a professional network within that industry. Create a step-by-step action plan: Plan your work and work your plan. Additionally, have a personal mission statement that defines your values and moral foundation, and ensure that every major decision aligns with this statement. Remember— people are watching!

▶ **Know when to take the plunge.** Timing is everything. Ensure that you plan and execute your exit strategy carefully when transitioning. Stay connected with your network to make your transition as seamless as possible. Understand the risks involved with changing jobs or starting a new business. Be aware of the potential downsides but be comfortable taking the plunge even without having all the answers. Remember, it's okay to ask for help—the upside can outweigh your fears![3]

When you reinvent yourself, it's important that you always present your very best self to the world. In this way, the people you meet will be left with the best impression of who you are and what you can do. The way I present myself to people, always showing the best of who I am, has made them believe in me and given them a better sense of who I am, what I'm about, the values that drive me, how curious and insightful I am, and how persistent I am about my work ethic.

These interactions have not only helped to shape people's opinions about who I am but also opened my eyes to new opportunities and challenged me as an entrepreneur to work in a different way or to move outside of my comfort zone.

But, at the end of the day, my career so far has been an evolution of my passion and interest and I have always had the support of my network. You can really have a fruitful, successful career—whether as an entrepreneur or someone working in corporate America—by following your passion. So long as you have the support of your network and the fundamental know-how and ability and core skills to get the right things done, you can succeed in most anything you put your mind to, whether that's a project or a career.

If you've got something going for you that will help you open a door, then by all means use it and walk through that door. There's the perfect chance for you to get in faster than someone else and prove that you're worth the hype that preceded you. You will have the opportunity to become the new status quo and set the bar high for those who follow. Give the person who put his or her social capital on the line by backing you zero reasons to regret doing so and a million reasons to take credit loudly and proudly for seeing your potential and affording you a platform on which to shine.

FOR REFLECTION

- Always work on improving yourself.

- Believe in yourself.

- Only look to yourself for motivation.

- Know where and how you add value. Make your value proposition clear.

- Quantify your contributions and accomplishments.

- Find the connections in your journey, bring them to life in your story, and get comfortable with articulating the evolution of you.

7

There's No Such Thing as Work-Life Balance

(Give 110 Percent to Whatever You Do)

'LL NEVER FORGET THE TIME I was invited to speak at an MBA conference at the S.C. Johnson Graduate School of Management at Cornell University. The day I was scheduled to fly to Cornell for the talk, I got swamped with work, failed to check in online, and arrived at the airport to find that the flight had been oversold. It was the last flight of the night, of course.

So, I decided to go home, get some rest, and rent a car the next morning so I could drive the nearly six hours to Cornell. I barely made it in time for my 11 a.m. program slot, but I gave an hour-long keynote speech that everyone loved. It was probably one of the best speeches I'd ever given. I was on a real high until I learned that Hurricane Sandy had hit the East Coast and my flight out of Syracuse had been canceled. I found myself faced with the possibility of being stuck at Cornell for several days in the aftermath of the storm.

Instead of turning in my rental car at the Syracuse airport, as I had originally planned, I decided to drive back home to New York City.

I was getting ready to hit the road when I checked in with my mom, who was in New York City with my children. She said, "Absolutely not! There's a reason they canceled all those flights. What if your car is blown off the road or a projectile crashes through the windshield? I don't want you driving back that distance in this weather by yourself!"

It hadn't registered with me how bad the storm was, but as I watched the television news, it became increasingly clear that Sandy's visit was going to be tragic. So, I stayed in Syracuse, forcibly separated from my children and feeling like a terrible parent on the very day that I had felt the rush of accomplishment from giving one of the best speeches of my life. While I was thankful that my children were safe, I sat there in Syracuse with my stomach reeling for four days, worrying about my children and praying that they would be safe inside our home—that the windows wouldn't shatter and that my basement wouldn't flood.

So much for work-life balance! My work caused me to be away from my children during one of the most devastating hurricanes in American history. I was feeling great one moment—in command of myself and my audience—and helpless and like a bad parent the next, desperate to get back home by any means possible.

So, do you stay home with your children because you fear the storm that's coming—a storm that may or may not be as bad as the weather forecasters think—or do you push forward and follow through on an important business commitment that an Ivy League university has contracted you to do? I followed through on my commitment but ended up feeling terrible when the implications of my decision became clear.

Over ten years ago, Katharine Weymouth, publisher and chief executive of *The Washington Post*, made a statement about the ongoing debate on work-life balance for women. I believe the idea behind her thoughts still holds true today:

"In addition to being publisher and chief executive of the newspaper division of The Washington Post Co., I'm a single mom with three kids (ages eight, eleven, and twelve), three dogs, two hamsters (actually, one escaped, so we're down to one), a guinea pig, and a rabbit. So, as the debate about work-life balance rages on, I can vouch that a woman can have both a family and a demanding, interesting job. But there is no balance." [4]

I agree with Katharine Weymouth. Work-life balance does not exist. Combining life with work is a constant juggling act, a series of choices—"yes" and "no"—and your success depends on how well you can integrate one into the other. People often ask me, "How do you do this—how do you keep such a busy and successful career going with two kids and everything that goes along with that?" As much as I wish I had an answer to that question, I don't. Like many people with successful careers, I have a great nanny, but I understand that it's not something that everyone can have or do. The struggles, the frustration, and the constant internal battle between the responsibilities of motherhood, womanhood, and business are very real, and they can sap the energy out of even the most energetic and highly motivated person.

MAILLIAN: MOTHERHOOD

What will have the greatest impact on my children? Being more present at home or being a strong professional example? To me, the answer is clear. Children aspire to be what they find inspirational and cool. I feel that I am a far better parent for being their personal inspiration and role model, showing them how to genuinely lead by example.

I grapple with this balancing act all the time. When I had only one business and only one child, my son came first, and I had enough flexibility in my schedule to run the winery, do my speaking engagements, sit on my boards, and go to the music and Little Gym classes with my six-month-old. But even though I was running my own business and doing all these other tasks, I found myself envying the women who would show up at the nursery school in their power suits to drop off their children and then head off in a car service to go to some big meeting. Although I would do that every once in a while, I was (let's be honest) envious of the women who had the high-power corporate gigs.

Lauren
MAILLIAN

WHAT I'VE LEARNED ABOUT BUSINESS FROM MY COLLEAGUES

Selene Cuffe, president and CEO of Heritage Link Brands, has been a great friend, supporter, and client. Our relationship is proof that many fruitful business relationships start without a clear purpose, as ours did seven years ago when I was speaking at a conference and she was building Heritage Link Brands. Fast-forward five years, and she would be pushing me to help her build that business once I decided to sell mine. Here is her advice for success in business:

1. Surround yourself with successful people.

2. Listen.

3. Say "thank you" to those who help you, even with the simple things in life.

4. The support of others has had the greatest impact on my own success.

But guess what? The women who had the high-power corporate gigs were envious of me because I could take time off and go to music class and Little Gym with my child.

So, where's the balance? Who wins?

There is no balance, and if you try to keep score based on who's more successful and who has a more fulfilled life, I don't feel like you can ever win. It's a rare day when I feel as though I'm succeeding both as a parent and as a professional.

I've never taken an extended period of time off from my work. While many of my colleagues will take six months off and travel the world between ventures, I've never done that. I've never had a time-out. Instead, I've carved out shorter periods that have allowed me to be contemplative and reflective, and to affirm that I'm still happy with the frenetic path I've been traveling on. These reflective times also provide me with opportunities to redefine and refine my path and what the journey ahead will entail if I ever feel overwhelmed or unsure.

I thought I was going to take one of those longer, more thoroughly contemplative sabbatical-like moments after Sugarleaf Vineyards. When I exited the winery, everyone wanted to know what I was going to do next. And I thought to myself that this was going to be the prime opportunity for me to take off a few months and to hang out with my children and smell the roses for a while. So, that's what I told people I was going to do next—I was going to be a full-time mom for a little bit and give them all the energy I could.

But that never happened.

Before I knew it, I transitioned to Luxury Market Branding and the venture fund, where I was working seventeen, eighteen, some-times nineteen hours a day, getting the fund up and running and launching two businesses at the same time. Add to this the speaking, the writing, and mommyhood. Even now, I haven't been able to seize the opportunity I had planned to hang out with my children like I thought I would. So I feel like I've achieved but not necessarily arrived. Not yet. I think it depends on how you integrate your work life into your personal life and how you integrate your personal life into your work life.

In a way, they're one and the same, but people constantly try to artificially divide them, even though employees today are expected to give far more of themselves to their work and business relationships than they did even a decade ago.

Having children hasn't really affected my career because I've always been an entrepreneur. With my first business, they were always nearby or attached to my hip. My career has progressed and become more demanding while my children have grown and matured. As more opportunities came my way, it was serendipitous that they were ready for nursery school, which gave me more free time to build my other companies.

It couldn't have worked out better, really. Motherhood influences my business decisions because I always want to make my children proud of me, my career, and my choices. I take great pride in instilling the values of hard work, persistence, and perseverance in my children. Having children is a humbling honor that reminds me every day that I have to stay true to myself and do what would make them proud years from now.

Again, it comes down to having the success you want. Many of my incredibly accomplished friends feel that because they're not yet married with children, they're not successful. Conversely, those who have a family often feel the sacrifices they've made to stay home don't always pay the dividends they expected. Define your success in a way that will fulfill you even if the factors and variables deviate from your plan.

I've recently found that sometimes that answer is easier to find when the question is rephrased as, "What makes me feel less guilty?" as opposed to "What will make me most happy?" Thankfully, my children don't pour on the guilt, so being a working mom doesn't make me feel unworthy as a parent. Entrepreneurs and people navigating their careers strive to balance both work and life concurrently as part of their plan for success. You are unlikely to strike a true balance, but you can craft what might be called a precarious relationship between the two. This requires constant tweaking and adjustment.

The most important way for entrepreneurs to maintain (or, gulp, salvage) romantic and social relationships while pursuing their career dreams is through effective communication with those whom they most care about and establishing ground rules that cannot be broken. It's hard to do well at work when your personal life is upside down and vice versa.

For me as an individual, and for many others in my generation who I see, interact with, advise, and invest in, we're not going to do well at work if we're not happy personally, and we're not going to do well personally if we're not happy at work. The two go hand in hand.

Learning to turn your brain off is a skill I have yet to master, but I'm working on it every day. Be fully present at work when you're at work, and be fully present at home when you're at home. In this day and age, when there is little separation between your work life and your personal life, it's crucial to learn how to turn off the work mode when it's time to be home or out with family and friends. You need to recharge your batteries so you can face the next day's work challenges with everything you've got.

It's key to know when to push forward with full force—to put on your work cap, get in the zone, and give 110 percent. But it's just as important to recognize that if you don't regularly unplug from work, burnout is likely. You need recovery time.

Like many entrepreneurs and businesspeople, my work often extends into my personal and vacation time, blurring the lines between work and play. This issue is particularly prevalent today, as technology increasingly blurs the line between work and home life.

Cloud networking software company Pertino published a study revealing that 64 percent of men confess to working while on vacation, and 57 percent of women admit to doing the same.

Over the past couple of years, vacations have often involved me working in between moments of relaxation. A prime example is my trip to the Cannes Lions Festival. While it was an exciting and enlightening experience for both me and my family, the primary reason for our presence there was business. I was representing the brand I served as president for at the time, and although we enjoyed the beautiful surroundings and vibrant energy of the festival, much of my focus was on fulfilling my professional responsibilities. Even in a setting as picturesque as Cannes, the demands of work were ever-present, proving once again that true separation between work and personal time is not the easiest to achieve.

My dilemma was a common one for businesspeople today, and I took the path that most of us end up taking: I brought my work along on vacation. It was the path of least resistance and maximum productivity.

I found myself setting up spaces for our events, meeting fellow entrepreneurs to discuss collaboration opportunities, and, of course, closing investment deals. I was literally sitting as close as I could to the Wi-Fi router in the hotel lobby, where I temporarily set up shop and completed all my closings using emails, confirming papers, and electronic signatures. Within a day, I was done with the work and could refocus my energy on my kids and some much-needed rest and relaxation.

I have no doubt that of those 57 percent of women in the Pertino study who admit to doing some work while on vacation, entrepreneurs make up the lion's share. Separating work time from leisure time has long been the entrepreneur's dilemma—in my experience, entrepreneurs and company owners work far more hours for themselves than do their employees.

This makes sense given that these people have some serious skin in the game—they own their businesses, most likely provided financing out of their own pockets, and so most deeply feel its successes and its failings. But I do think that this dilemma is increasingly becoming a problem for everyone—not only for entrepreneurs but also for those who work in corporate jobs. While top companies have always expected employees to work long hours, now the common expectation is not merely to work long hours but to be in touch 24/7.

Here's how I approach the dilemma: Is it better to do a little bit of work while you're away, or is it better to completely unplug, come back recharged, and tackle everything upon return?

For me, the latter choice always seems like a lose-lose because a few days out of the email loop can result in missing out on important discussions and decision-making opportunities. Or, worse, you return to find a conversation that's been bounced around and now has fifteen different replies for you to sift through. It often feels like it takes an extra three days just to catch up after returning from an unplugged vacation. At least, that's been my experience, with voicemails, emails, and everything else piling up.

So, I've developed a few strategies to deal with this dilemma. Here are some approaches you can try on your next vacation:

> **Employ the email fake-out**: I use a little trick with my email that's surprisingly effective (but don't tell anyone!). When I inform people that I'm about to leave for vacation, I let them believe I'll be gone an extra day or two longer than I actually will be. This way, I avoid getting overwhelmed with messages and calls on my first day back and have a bit of time to catch up on my inbox and voicemails.

➤ **Say goodbye to your laptop**: I've started experimenting with leaving my laptop behind on vacation, relying only on my phone and an iPad. This doesn't completely eliminate work, but it significantly limits what I can do. I can keep up with essential messages, but I'm less tempted to dive into creating or modifying documents, which I might be inclined to do if my laptop were with me.

➤ **Use an email autoresponder**: Setting up an email autoresponder is crucial. This simple tool helps manage expectations about your availability and reduces the pressure to respond immediately. A well-crafted autoresponder lets people know when you're away and sets a clear timeline for when you'll be back, helping to manage both your workload and your peace of mind.

➤ **Make an appointment with your work**: Rather than letting work take over your vacation, allocate specific times for it. Set clear boundaries and stick to them. If you can't be highly productive or contribute meaningfully in the time you've set aside, it can wait. If you have kids, consider working when they're asleep. If you're traveling with a partner, early mornings might be the best time to handle work so you can enjoy quality time together during the day.

➤ **Be flexible.** Remember: you're on vacation for a reason—to unplug from the frenetic work scene for a while and to relax and take some time to think about what's most important in your life.

Generation Y doesn't measure success and happiness strictly in terms of salary and title—there's much more to it than that. Its members want to make a meaningful impact and change the world, or at least to have an impact on the lives of those around them. And it's also true that high performers of any generation want to work with other high performers, which makes it especially important to keep your best people happy with their jobs and their employers.

The average time that a Gen Y employee stays in his or her job is little more than two years (Gen X is for five years and Baby Boomers for seven years), so you've got to do something above and beyond to retain your Gen Y talent. (Also interesting is the finding that only 36 percent of Gen Y males and females list a job or company on their Facebook profiles, while 80 percent of this same group lists at least one school on their profile.)

A few years ago, I wrote an article for *Fast Company* magazine, "5 Tips to Retaining Star Gen Y Talent." Although the topic of the article is aimed at working with Gen Y employees, the tips in the article may apply to any high-performing employee of any age. The prime work environment for the top-performing minds will have the characteristics outlined below to support the needs and interests of this holy grail of today's talent.

If they sacrifice what they are looking for in a work environment—whether they are building an ecosystem for their own team or looking to be employed in an established workplace—these attributes will ensure that they have the best chance of thriving and accelerating their careers on their own terms.

Don't accept mediocrity. And take advantage of the many companies that are building company cultures to allow you to evolve as an individual. No shrinking violets allowed!

If you follow the below advice, you are certain to create goodwill between your organization and its Gen Y rock stars, while you help put your Gen Y employees squarely on the path to success. And don't forget: This advice is applicable to any high-performing employee, not only your Gen Y people. When your employees succeed, so too will your company—and, by extension, you.

- **Be transparent.** Gen Y values honesty. Tell them clearly what you need them to complete before they can do something interesting or lead a project. They're motivated by working toward the bigger goal, seeing the opportunity to take a bigger path, and developing the next steps. There's no motivation for them otherwise. Gen Y values openness in communication, and they are resilient.

- **Explain the bigger purpose.** Contextualize your organization's social and environmental values. Gen Y wants (and needs) to change the world's path toward sustainability and social good.

- **Provide opportunities for professional development.** Gen Y employees want to grow onward, and they eventually want to steer the ship. They want to see the next steps, understand the reference points, and talk about how to get there and get it done. They want to master being effective professionals and they enjoy the development process. Arm them with responsibility and watch them thrive under the guise of your "big picture." It may not be perfect, but they will undoubtedly provide a fresh perspective and may even spark a new idea. [And remember: This doesn't necessarily mean that you've got to spend a bunch of money on leadership or other training programs. Delegating effectively is a good strategy for professional development, and it won't cost you or your business a dime.]

▶ **Understand that Gen Y views career as life.** Work-life integration is the new work-life balance. Gen Y is a hyper-communicative, constantly "on" generation that always expects a response and can easily transition from personal to professional at the speed of a tweet. To them, their career is life and life is their career—it's one and the same, and this can be a great thing for your company.

▶ **Give them opportunities to shine in the community.** Support your employees' work and relationships with outside organizations [and nonprofits and other causes] that they are passionate about. Appreciate the fact that they want to add value to organizations other than your company and view it positively. After all, their involvement in outside organizations may even open doors for your company. Allow them to be dynamic individuals—it builds their resume and will make your company more cultured.

Remember: It's the person, not the degree or the resume, that gets hired. Having a polished skill set is important, but getting hired often comes down to your network, and it comes down to people wanting to work with people they know, like, and trust. When you're going to spend almost one-third of your life with someone on the job, you want that to be as enjoyable and painless as possible.

So most times, people will choose a business partner or a company will hire an employee based on who he or she is and what they represent more than on a person's resume or degree. Getting hired (and staying employed) comes down to your skills, experience, perspective, and your ability to execute and build value.

If you feel as though a candidate has the right basic qualities as an individual, you can teach that person the few job skills he or she lacks. You can't teach a candidate to be a better person, however, or to be more committed or have more passion. You can't teach a candidate to be more energetic or a multitasker who's happy to step outside a comfort zone to take on new projects and tasks that aren't explicitly outlined in a job description.

These aren't teachable skills. They're learnable skills but not teachable skills. Someone can choose to learn them over time, but they're rarely something that you can walk into a situation and just be taught. Gen Y and Gen X employees yearn to be independent and to leave their regular jobs behind. This makes your job of retaining them that much more challenging. A recent survey found that 72 percent of Millennials in "regular" jobs want to be entirely independent, and 61 percent plan to be independent within two years.

"Freedom" was the number one reason for wanting to leave their conventional careers behind and work for themselves. In addition, working wherever they like (92 percent), working whenever they like (87 percent), working on more interesting projects (69 percent), and traveling while working (50 percent preferred this to vacation time) were also strong motivators.

To be totally honest, there are times when I really do think it's important for me to be as unplugged as I possibly can be—especially when I'm on vacation with my family. I recently had the opportunity to push myself on this when I took a brief vacation trip to Morocco (and checked another item off my bucket list). For this trip, I decided to take the first baby step toward putting this idea of getting unplugged into practice by taking only my iPad along with me and leaving my laptop behind. If I couldn't get it done on my iPad, then it would have to wait until I got back.

I survived, my business partners survived, and my clients survived. In fact, we all did fine. Plus, I actually was able to focus on seeing the wondrous sites of Marrakech and beyond instead of continually messing with my laptop. I knew I would have been upset with myself if, instead of taking time to explore the Medina, enjoy the unique culture, and take beautiful photographs, I sat by the pool with my laptop catching up on emails and drafting business plans and pitches. What's the point? What are you trying to be successful for if your family isn't happy and you aren't happy? It's easy to lose sight of what's most important if you don't watch yourself.

FOR REFLECTION

- Find a flow and exchange of work/personal time that optimizes your ideal work-life integration.

- Work where you'll thrive and where those in charge are willing to support all of your interests.

- The more demanding your professional life is, the more you must err on the side of over-communication in your personal life to be successful.

- Measure your success based on your level of happiness and positive impact on others.

8

Claim It and Shine

(Leverage Is What Makes You Different)

BELIEVE THAT EVERYONE HAS SOMETHING—
SOME personal characteristic—that will open doors. Some
people are naturally intelligent, and this opens certain doors for them,
while other people are persistent, assertive, or have some influence
over the people in power. Others are charming, charismatic, or can
tell a great story—these things make them unique, open doors, and
create opportunities for them.

What personal characteristics do you possess that make you
unique and attract the attention of others?

Recognize what it is that creates opportunities for you. I always
find it interesting that when it comes to this topic, people often
want to ignore the elephant in the room: that they might have some

characteristics that give them a leg up on their competition—both outside of an organization and within it. But it is what it is.

So what does this elephant in the room look like?

It could be that you're a woman and there aren't many women in your chosen field. Or it could be because you're a man and there aren't that many men in that position. Or you might be the subject of attention because you're new, different, or stand out from the crowd in some other way. It could even be that your parents, boyfriend, or spouse are well-connected, and someone in their network wants to return a favor. Whatever it is, when the door opens, take that opportunity and run with it.

It doesn't matter why the door opens. If it opens, don't hesitate to walk through it.

Don't play only the position others feel you're capable of. Show that you're capable of doing so much more, especially when you aren't specifically asked or required to do so. If you've got drive, tenacity, and you look adversity in the face and shine, then show it. For example, I have a level of erudition that surprises people, disarms any stereotypes they may have had, and forces them to change their opinions about me. It makes me stand out from the crowd, and I know it—and I don't hesitate to show it.

Are you prepared to grab your opportunity by the collar when it calls your name? In some cases, you might not even understand what it is that makes someone want to give you a break or take you under their wing. That person might see a bit of herself in you, or maybe she sees your potential as a rising star in the industry before you can see it for yourself. Again, the reason someone decides to give you an opportunity doesn't matter. What matters is that you step up and take it. It's your time to shine.

Don't be ashamed of your successes. More importantly, don't allow someone to discredit your successes. Winners never quit.

Quitters never win. Never underestimate your ability to persevere without a partner. Never look outside yourself for motivation.

I received a lot of attention back when I started Gen Y Capital Partners—fortunately, most of it positive. Other firms and big players in the space found out that a woman who was less than thirty years old—me, Lauren Maillian—was starting a venture firm, and in a very short time, people were making a big deal about it.

I duly noted the fact, and then I owned it and leveraged it to my advantage. The fact that I did those things when I was very young had nothing to do with why I helped start up Gen Y Capital Partners. But I did stand out from the crowd of other VCs, and I was not afraid to use personal characteristics to open doors and create more opportunities for myself. Once that door is open—even a crack—I walk right on through.

So you might ask, "Why would the founder of a winery decide to make the move to venture capital?" It's a good question. I can't imagine two kinds of businesses that are any farther apart from each other in terms of operations, pacing, and culture. They really are apples and oranges. Wine vintages are measured in years, while VC deals can sometimes go down in hours or even minutes.

MAILLIAN: LEVERAGING WHAT MAKES YOU DIFFERENT

It doesn't matter why the door opens. If it opens, don't hesitate to walk through it, but be prepared to work harder than expected. Expectations of you are always higher than they may outwardly seem.

I saw a lot of opportunity in venture capitalism. And, believe it or not, money was the least motivating factor in my decision to start the firm. What got me excited was the breadth of experience that I wanted to have—my finger on the pulse of what is a very innovative field. I knew the venture world was going to be a continuously changing and evolving landscape that would always combine the competitive, the innovative, and the cool. And that has definitely turned out to be the case.

Ask yourself, "Why will I win?" and "Why will I succeed?" What is it that makes you stand out from the crowd? Why are you unique? If you're currently in business—whether as an entrepreneur or otherwise—you are probably well aware of the importance of differentiating your product from others like it in the marketplace. When consumers are looking at an array of buying possibilities within a particular product category, say computers, shoes, or automobiles, they want to know what makes your product special and why it's a better option for them than the similar products offered by your competitors. Does it look better?

Does it last longer? Is it faster? Is it less expensive? Does it offer better value over the long run? The answers to these questions and others like them all add up to the specific characteristics that differentiate your products in the marketplace.

WHAT I'VE LEARNED ABOUT BUSINESS FROM MY COLLEAGUES

1. Figure out what you love and are good at and excel. Determine where you are less strong and surround yourself with people who round out your capacity.

2. Carve out even a little time every day to be creative and think boldly and strategically. To do this, leave your office, turn off your phone, and step away from the computer.

3. Be kind, generous, and welcoming to everyone—offer help wherever you can. Be just as thoughtful about asking for what you need.

—CHLOE DREW, *Chief People Officer, Redox*

Similarly, you can and should differentiate yourself or your brand from the competition to land a new client or promotion, for example, or to attract the venture funding you seek. Take time to consider: What do you bring to the table that's going to attract someone's attention? Remember: Sometimes you need to attract that attention for the brief moment it takes to get your foot in the door and make your pitch. And when you make your pitch, you'll be able to further differentiate yourself from the competition.

Dress for success—not only personally but also for your business. If you run a fashion company and your website isn't beautiful—crisp, clean, or gorgeous—then you're going to have a big problem with prospective clients. When I see a sloppy company website, I personally wouldn't trust you to have the level of expertise necessary for me to want to work with you.

Part of dressing for success is dressing like you belong. If you show up for a job interview at a fashion business and claim you're a designer, yet you're not wearing something uniquely designed or created—preferably by you—then I'm not going to take you seriously.

Years ago, people would meet me, and they couldn't imagine that I knew how to run a winery and create and market an award-winning product. But I did. And sometimes people look at me and can't imagine that I was tapped to help start up a venture fund. But I was. The moment people got past the surface of what I look like and once they heard what I had to say, they were often in for a big surprise: I am a very talented businessperson who knows her stuff.

Which brings me to another question: What's your personal elevator pitch?

I've worked for years with all sorts of start-ups, helping companies figure out how to pitch to investors. In the start-up world, a well-thought-out and polished elevator pitch is essential. The perfect pitch is a few minutes long. And in that time, you need to describe:

- ➤ Who you are
- ➤ What your business is
- ➤ What your goals are
- ➤ Your vision for the future.

The perfect elevator pitch gets your foot in the door—it's designed to pique your audience's curiosity and make them eager to learn more about your opportunity.

In the context of an individual, your personal elevator pitch should do much the same. It should succinctly convey who you are, what you do, what your goals are, and your vision for the future. It should inspire your audience to want to know more about you and imagine how you might align with their own goals and visions for the future.

What's your pitch? If you have a small window of opportunity and the door opens for you just a crack, what will you say or do to make yourself stand out and shine? To make jaws drop?

I think it's important to reach out to people who are more accomplished than you are. Ann Friedman wrote a great post on NYMag. com titled "Shine Theory: Why Powerful Women Make the Greatest Friends." It suggests that women should go out of their way to be better friends with one another, embracing the successes of female friends and colleagues instead of expressing jealousy.

It reminds us to seek out successful women in our networks because their successes may often become our successes as well— and there's power in these connections. These successful women can sometimes open doors for us, provide valuable insights, help elevate our careers, or amplify our thoughts and opinions in larger arenas.

There's a cyclical effect when you have smart, amazing, powerful women in your networks who are readily available—whether as best friends, sounding boards, mentors, or advisors. Through my professional journey, I have discovered not only who I am but also who my supporters and confidants are. We push each other to greatness.

I am extremely grateful for the networks of amazing women I have around me because, believe me, it hasn't always been that way. Honestly, it's only been within the last four or five years that I have built these networks of accomplished women in the marketing, media, and start-up communities. I consider them not only colleagues but friends because, to me, they're one and the same. If I decided to start a new company tomorrow or needed members for a new advisory board, these are the people I would turn to. They are already in my circle, my tribe—that's the power of sisterhood.

WHAT I'VE LEARNED ABOUT BUSINESS FROM MY COLLEAGUES

Donna Williams, Chief Audience Development Officer for the Metropolitan Museum of Art, gave me the following advice for someone who wants to be successful:

1. Know who you are—understand your weaknesses and strengths.
2. Be clear and focused about your objectives.
3. Be willing to step out on a limb if necessary to achieve your goals and realize that everyone can make a difference.

Kathleen Warner, former Chief Operating Officer of Startup America Partnership (SUAP), had an impressive career. As COO of SUAP, a significant part of her role was staying attuned to the pulse of entrepreneurship and exploring how she and SUAP could fuel its growth. Early on, Kathleen confided in me about wrapping up Startup America and sought my perspective on her next steps.

Kathleen has a diverse background—she's been involved in politics and is an attorney, though she hasn't practiced in years. The questions for her were: Should she return to the political world? Go back to practicing law? Continue in the nonprofit sector? Or explore her newfound passion in the entrepreneurial or start-up space?

I encouraged Kathleen to remain in the start-up community, where she had recently planted her roots and shown great passion. I told her that, as a natural leader—passionate, driven, and experienced in growing companies—I saw her continuing in a COO role or another executive position. Her broad experience is rare in the start-up world. She could leverage her core skills in operations management and combine them with her legal background to guide a growth-stage start-up. This, I believed, would allow Kathleen to experience the rewards of entrepreneurship both hands-on and through an equity stake. I envisioned her in a growth-stage company where she could witness tangible progress, something that typically takes much longer in the law or nonprofit sectors.

I discussed potential introductions and opportunities for her entrepreneurial leadership journey. I told her candidly that, given her talents and passions, this was the path she should pursue at this point in her life. I aimed to get her excited about her future in ways she hadn't considered, and I think I convinced her to explore a more entrepreneurial route—time will tell! It would be easy for Kathleen to return to familiar fields like law or politics, but she has developed new passions, expertise, and a new network. I'm confident this is where her spirit and path will lead her.

So, why should I bother helping people like Kathleen? Simply put, it makes me happy. If I'm in a position to assist a friend and colleague, why wouldn't I? Maybe next time, I'll be the one needing help or advice.

Bruce Kasanoff wrote a compelling blog post in May 2013 titled "Three Words That Will Transform Your Career." The three words? Help this person. Kasanoff argues, "Every time you encounter another person, think: Help this person. It's not altruistic. Nothing can so quickly supercharge your career and improve the quality of your life."[5]

He goes on to describe various everyday situations that often frustrate us—waiting in a long line for coffee at Starbucks, being constantly interrupted by phone calls during a busy workday, or dealing with an underperforming employee. Instead of approaching these situations with a negative mindset, Kasanoff suggests viewing them through the lens of "help this person" and then acting accordingly.

For instance, rather than getting frustrated with the coffee barista, try to make her smile instead. Remember, she's managing a constant stream of impatient customers. Instead of letting your frustration affect the way you handle phone calls during your busy day, focus on addressing the needs of the caller. And rather than criticizing the employee who isn't performing up to par, help him find the training he needs or a position within your organization that better aligns with his skills and interests.

Not only do you assist others by changing your attitude and approach, but you also benefit yourself. You become a more positive, proactive, and constructive person—the kind of individual successful people want to hire and work with and the kind high performers aspire to work for. Adopting these three simple words can profoundly impact your life and those around you.

When Kathleen Warner and I met for drinks, I had no idea a transition was on the horizon for her. Once I learned about her situation, I knew I had to give her my honest, unvarnished advice. I outlined the upsides and downsides of the various opportunities before her, aiming to provide fresh data points she could consider in her decision-making process. My main goal was to help her choose the path that would bring her the most happiness.

The key to a valuable personal advisory circle is surrounding yourself with individuals who have no ulterior motives, hidden agendas, or anything to gain or lose by being honest. Kathleen knows I am one of those people, and the friends and colleagues in my inner circle know this too.

FOR REFLECTION

- Find your unique characteristic and make it your trademark.
- Acknowledge the elephant in the room to facilitate meaningful conversations.
- Don't let anyone discredit your successes.
- Always know the answers to these questions: Why will I win? Why will I succeed?
- Don't be afraid to seize opportunities where they arise.
- Have your personal elevator pitch ready at all times.
- Surround yourself with people who will lift you up.

9

Be Deliberate

(Put Your Emotions Aside)

'M OFTEN ASKED WHY I left behind my first major business success—Sugarleaf Vineyards. It's the romantic kind of business that many people dream of owning and enjoying. I left it because I had built what I considered to be the best business I possibly could—I had achieved all of my goals far sooner than I had anticipated.

I realized that we were at the peak of our value given the physical constraints of the business and that further growth in value would not happen without making another massive financial investment into expanding the business physically. A physical expansion would have meant boosting the capacity of the winery production, expanding the tasting room to accommodate more customers, and making other major—and expensive—improvements to move the business to the next level.

When a situation like this occurs, an entrepreneur is forced to weigh the various options available. Is it better to stick around and grow the business, which will require both cash and recovery time— that is, the time it will take to recover and recoup the additional money you've expended? Or is it better to exit when you're on top and everything is going your way?

As I write these words, I realize how much this is like deciding whether or not to ask the dealer in a game of 21 to hit your hand one last time or hold. Asking for another card exposes you to the risk of going higher than twenty-one and losing the hand, while sticking with the hand you've been dealt is the safer, but potentially lower payoff, route to take. Sometimes the only way to get what you sincerely want in life requires leaving behind the sure thing you already have.

Although I had achieved my goals, it wasn't an easy decision for me to make. By then, our wines had been served in the White House and at the 2010 Governor's Ball, and the buzz around our brand was growing by leaps and bounds.

We had received tons of press about the winery and our wines, as well as about me as a young rising star in the industry. It was an intoxicating position to be in, and it would have been easy for me to lower my aspirations and simply hunker down at Sugarleaf, staying safely within the comfort zone that insulated me from the inevitable ups and downs of the rough-and-tumble world of business start-ups.

Many people build businesses for a lifestyle they are attached to, one that allows them to kick back and collect a check, which is where I found myself with the winery. I still worked in the winery, but my days of schmoozing with customers in the tasting room and rolling up my sleeves were over. I wasn't getting behind the bar, ringing up sales, or putting wine in bottles. I would do it if I was there, but it had gotten to the point where I didn't have to do that anymore—I had employees who took care of those day-to-day tasks.

Good entrepreneurs know when to extract the most value from what they've built, but I learned that I was way too emotionally attached to the winery to extract anything. I wanted my children, Jayden and Chloe, to get married there after all—it was something I had dreamed about and longed for.

Fortunately, my entrepreneur friends didn't hesitate to pull my head out of the clouds and bring me back down to earth. They sat me down, looked me in the eyes, and said, "Are you serious, Lauren? You're going to hang on to this business only because you want your children to get married there in twenty or twenty-five years?"

When I thought about the winery this way, I realized that holding onto it and sinking a permanent anchor deep into my comfort zone would eventually destroy my spirit. But at the time, I guess I had never really envisioned my life any other way.

I was reminded by my circle of close friends that I wasn't going to be happy if I didn't continue to build something new. But I didn't know what that something was—I didn't know what I wanted. I'm someone who's usually very clear about what I want—except in this one particular case. I worked to build the winery to the point where I would be able to enjoy my summers in Italy doing "business develop-ment and market research"—aka tasting wines in Tuscany. But I was on autopilot with the business, and it was no longer a challenge, fun, or exciting. It was slowly driving me crazy.

Have you ever been in the position of having to decide between sticking with something safe and familiar, or leaving that behind for an opportunity that could turn out quite differently? If you have, you know the excitement of taking on a new challenge—and the anxiety of not knowing what the outcome will be. But perhaps even more important: Have you shied away from taking on a new challenge because you were afraid that you might fail? If so, what was the outcome? Did your decision turn out to be a good one, or are you forever looking back, wishing you had made a change in your life when you had the chance?

There is no shortage of opportunities out there in this wide world. What there is a shortage of is talented, hardworking people who do what they say they are going to do. If you are one of these rare people, you will never have a problem attracting opportunities.

MAILLIAN: BEING DELIBERATE

> There is no shortage of opportunities out there in this wide world. What there is a shortage of is talented, hardworking people who do what they say they are going to do.

So far, every decision I've made about my career has been the result of some incredible opportunity coming to me—it's never been because I chased an opportunity. Opportunities come to me because of my experience, expertise, networks, and the kind of person I am. I bring something special to every project I work on and to every client I work with. I bring me—110 percent of Lauren. When I'm in, I'm all in. Be sure to bring 100 percent of yourself—110 percent if you can manage it—to every interaction, meeting, and call during the course of your day. Be an expert, build a network, and bring something special to every project you work on and every client you work with.

In my experience, success comes to those who do the following:

▶ Tap into whatever it is that gets you most excited about life.

▶ Leverage and bring to the table the very best of what you have to offer—every day of the week.

▶ Understand it's not about acting like a man or a woman—it's about being yourself and proving yourself and your tenacity. It's about doing more than most would expect, better than anyone would imagine, repeatedly.

▶ Make big promises and bold statements, and live by them, or bust your ass trying to figure out how you'll make it make sense and ultimately work. Even if it doesn't turn out as you envisioned, enough people will notice how hard you worked, how relentless you were, how much persistence you had, and ultimately how you persevered. The process, regardless of the outcome, is priceless. I do it every day.

There isn't just one approach to success in business for women. That said, certain tactics, strategies, and approaches are more likely to get you to where you want to be. Your job is to figure out which tactics, strategies, and approaches are right for you, and then to pursue them with a single-minded passion. Know your audience and how to communicate with them to get what you need.

Lauren Maillian (signature)

WHAT I'VE LEARNED ABOUT BUSINESS FROM MY COLLEAGUES

Morin Oluwole is the embodiment of creating opportunity by outworking others to achieve success. She's incredibly smart and well-educated and has been committed to gaining as much experience in complementary areas of management and operations since she joined Facebook. Oluwole pushed through every difficult experience while never losing sight of her goals. Here's her advice on business:

4. Relationships matter the most—take time to cultivate them.

5. Always be open to learning—there is someone who knows more than you.

6. Confidence is everything. Fake it until you make it.

7. The support of an incredible network of peers, colleagues, advisors, champions, friends, family—and even naysayers— has had an indelible impact on my personal and professional success.

—MORIN OLUWOLE, *Board Director, Global Luxury & Digital Strategy Advisor*

Do your homework, research the individual, get familiar with their background, and determine ahead of time why you'd like their attention. Be deliberate in your communication and assertive. Remember the elevator pitch discussion from Chapter 8?

When you get someone's attention, be direct, and don't waste their time. Most of the time, you've only got two minutes to say, "Hi, my name is Susan. This is where I'm from. This is what I'm working on. This is what I admire about you, and I was wondering if you had a few moments to discuss something I think you'll be interested in."

When it comes to women, it seems that two stereotypes prevail. The first is that women are timid and don't know what they want. The second stereotype—at the other end of the spectrum—is that very forward, overly aggressive women will boss everyone around until they get what they want.

Here are my suggestions for women (really, for anyone) who want to show their true selves to the world and not be stereotyped by others:

- Be direct, deliberate, poised, and assertive without being aggressive.

- Learn to clearly communicate in a way that commands respect but isn't abrasive.

- Be concise and contextualize your main points or objectives. When people need additional details, provide them, but don't overload them with minutiae.

- Be self-aware. This will align your strengths with organizational needs while helping you mitigate your weaknesses, creating a confidence that will inspire others. A success-oriented outlook on life and work is contagious.

- Always be committed to the job at hand. Do it well and get noticed enough to move forward.

► Don't let being ambitious make you cold. Know that you can be likable while being competitive and then learn to do it well.

Frankly, there aren't a lot of women out there funding start-ups. Men still dominate the ranks of VCs, and they write most of the checks. But getting funded by the boys' club doesn't mean that you've got to start acting like a man. In my experience, however, it does mean that you've got to start thinking in a less emotional, more clinical, analytical, and black-and-white way, which successful men tend to employ in their own thought processes. The most successful men I know check their emotions at the door when they come to work.

So, what can women do to command respect, attention, and professional admiration from the influential men in their industry? And how can you become the woman at the top of the list with the boys' club in your given business or industry?

Jeremy Johnson, entrepreneur and the co-founder and CEO of Andela, outlined some of the reasons he wanted to work with me. Have you checked similar boxes?

I wanted to work with [Lauren] because the strongest teams require competing viewpoints and real counterweights. [Her] poise and practicality permeate [her] interactions, and [her] professional accomplishments have consistently reinforced that. I needed someone who could push back against the vision and force it to collide with reality in a way that few people who favor reality are capable of doing.

To that point, [she is] successful because, while many people can live in either the present or the future, [she] seeks the future while filtering it through the lens of the present, a remarkably rare approach to the world. [She's] comfortable with operations, which requires an inherent appreciation for how things are, while also being open to changing them and exploring how they might be. The most successful dreamers are only successful because they find someone with that skill set to balance their pursuits and proposals.

Further, [she is] also successful because [she] cares deeply about both what [she] does and how [she] does it. One of the smartest people I've ever known told me that how you do anything is how you do everything. [Lauren] seeks to do everything well and un-abashedly throws [herself] into any new endeavor or pursuit with the knowledge that [her] work product will be world-class . . .

Whether we like it or not, there aren't as many women with the clout that these highly successful men have. While I'm confident that this situation will change in time, we're not there yet. We have to deal with the reality we are faced with, not the fantasy of some desired future state. But if we always bring the best of ourselves to every meeting, every conversation, every deal, we can earn the respect, attention, and professional admiration of the most highly successful people in any industry.

Not through any particular preference on my part to forge trails for women in business, I've entered three industries that have been domi-nated by men—the wine industry, marketing, and the world of venture capital. While each of these industries does already have women who play important roles within them, each has been dominated by men for decades, and even centuries. And, of course, the fact that I am a woman makes my entry into these industries much more of a rarity.

Be all in all the time, personally and professionally. That's how I am; it's the only way I know how to be. I'm an all-or-nothing kind of person with my relationships—I love hard. I'm either 110 percent on board, excited, dedicated, and passionate about a project, client, board seat, or an investment or advisory role, or I politely decline because I know that I'm not going to be able to give it everything I've got.

The point is, when you look at your opportunities, relationships, networks, or anything else that you're thinking of getting involved in, you've got to assess each one to see if it's something you're going to be all in about. If you're not, then you shouldn't pursue it. Don't pursue things when you know you won't want to be all in.

Remember: The very thing that you may be most self-conscious and uncomfortable about is likely your unique trump card that will set you apart from the pack and make you memorable. Never feel ashamed or undeserving because an opportunity became available to you easier or faster than it did to others because of something that makes you unique.

When you get noticed faster or are given access sooner, it often means that you will be expected to work harder and smarter and deliver results that are consistent with your personal values and reputation, surpassing what is commonly believed you are capable of. So, whatever you did to attract and accelerate an opportunity toward you is also, in many cases, the same thing that increases the expectations others have for you to succeed with that opportunity.

Who you know might get your foot in the door, but I can guarantee that no business will keep you around for very long if you don't perform. No company can afford to carry deadweight for long, and no one makes it to the top of the mountain without climbing. No man or woman keeps their place in the work arena if they don't belong. And no one belongs who isn't making a meaningful impact and measurable contribution of impressive quality—period!

Let no one discredit the successes on your journey, least of all yourself.

FOR REFLECTION

- Be confident and firm in your decisions.

- Always keep the bigger goal top of mind.

- Be assertive, clear, and confident, especially when time is of the essence.

- Remember that you either "come in" with what you want or you "earn" it—strategize how you'll achieve your goals.

- Let no one discredit your journey.

10

Always Push Ahead

(Use Your Tears to Move Through the Obstacles)

YOU CAN FIND STRENGTH IN the most unexpected places. When I was going through my divorce, I experienced a brief period where I wanted to sleep until I could wake up and it would all be over. I felt defeated and hopeless. I questioned who I was and the path my life had taken. I wasn't motivated to get up and out of the house to do anything, and it was difficult for me to find the motivation or confidence that I needed to push forward.

Then, a dear friend, who is like a second mom to me, gave me a paperback copy of *Eat, Pray, Love* by Elizabeth Gilbert. Inside the front and back covers, she wrote the following:

My dearest Lauren,

Please know that even in our darkest hour, we only have twenty-four hours in a day, and then a new day is upon us. And weeping may endure for a night, but joy comes in the morning. I pray that you cross that bridge over troubled waters, that your tears serve as a faucet of new perspective toward true happiness and fulfillment. My prayers for you are to end the poisonous disruptions that are causing suffering to you and everyone who cares about you.

I support the realization of purpose, passion, and truth for you.

Re-evaluate your self-worth and let not worldly treasures offer up a discount. Place your pride and dignity on a pedestal that cannot be dethroned. Present your "infit" as others perceive your outfit. Refuse any and all offers to place a price on your self-respect and self-worth, for they are immeasurable and simply cannot be purchased. I love you deeply, like a daughter born from my heart rather than my body. I am hurt when you are hurt, but I am strong when you falter. You are beautiful, special, worthy, and highly desirable . . . flaws and all.

Let's prepare to receive your blessings moving forward. Treat yourself with optimal care, and all others will have no option but to do the same. Restore the boundaries that once existed but now seem erased. Reset the compass of morality that perhaps has been buried under our designer lifestyles. Fall in love with yourself, and others will follow suit. Flaunt your victories of overcoming obstacles, hurdles, struggles, and trials and tribulations.

This, too, will pass.

I received the book on July 31, 2010. And I think it was on the very next day—August 1, 2010—that I finally found the strength I needed to pull myself up out of the funk I was in and promised to never again go backward into that abyss. It was time to push forward and get going. And I've been going strong ever since.

Setbacks and uncertainties can define who you are if you let them, and how your network of friends, family, and colleagues treats and embraces you during your hardships often defines how they think of you. It's the ultimate litmus test.

One of the most difficult lessons I've learned in my personal life, which transcends into business every day, is this: When someone shows you their true colors, believe them. Even harder and more difficult to do is to swiftly and tactfully extricate yourself from those people and situations before they prove themselves and their associations to be more toxic than fruitful.

WHAT I'VE LEARNED ABOUT BUSINESS FROM MY COLLEAGUES

1. **Always, always be yourself.** Life is not a race but a marathon—it takes less energy to "do you" than to "do someone else."

2. **Be generous and nice.** You never know who's watching.

3. **Your work ethic is key to your success.**

—**KATHRYN FINNEY,** *Founder of digitalundivided*

This has been incredibly hard for me to do—to trust and stay firm in my decisions and never look back. It's powerful to be disciplined, and making decisions you feel confident about is liberating.

Why do I stress having integrity and making it a top priority for those you choose to surround yourself with? Because I learned a hard lesson one time too many, but thankfully early on, that you can only take someone at their word. I've loaned money and never gotten it back. I've done favors that have been taken for granted. I've gone into business with someone who has proven that they cannot be trusted.

Here's the secret I've learned: People who value their own integrity wouldn't do such dishonorable things. The problem is that in today's world, people who truly possess such integrity and morality are hard to come by, so keep them in your inner circle when you stumble upon them.

One Sunday, my pastor offered up a piece of wisdom that has helped me through many moments of frustration, especially during the toughest personal battles of my adulthood. He said, "I have often regretted my words but never my silence." These words made me stronger and carried me through because there is a time and place for speech and actions and a time to remain silent. Silence can speak volumes.

Remain graceful and humble through the ups and the downs while staying true to your roots, and never lose sight of who you are deep down inside. Those who are watching the trajectory of your career will remember if you lost sight of who you are on your way up and how you acted when you thought you were on your way down. It will reflect how they think about you as a professional.

You don't always have to move up to find the success you're looking for. Many successful people have accepted new jobs that weren't as senior as the ones they previously had. They do this because they want to open up a new world of opportunities. You need to learn how to evaluate what serves you and your mission best. Is it working your way up the corporate ladder, or are you able to create the success you desire as an entrepreneur—better, faster, sooner? If you are able to hone a methodology for calculating your own decisions, it will carry you through your career. You'll always be able to weigh what's most important to you and be true to what you know defines your success.

MAILLIAN: PUSHING AHEAD

If the cup isn't half full, then add water.

I have found that people often go against what they feel in their heart, or what they feel is the right thing to do, because of outside pressure, be it from a boss, family member, or peer. But if you trust that your intuition will provide you with a strong indication of whether or not you're going in the right direction, you'll be happier with yourself for actually making that decision.

I don't often get an opportunity to say, "Okay, well, let me look into this and get back to you." So when my intuition tells me that I should take on a new opportunity or venture, I know that I have to do it. And I think this is one reason people want to work with me. They know that if I'm passionate about an opportunity and see value, I will figure out a way to make it happen and be a fully present and willing contributor. These things make me more of an asset, which increases the probability that the project will succeed. You must do this too if you want to succeed.

Let's rewind for a moment to when I started the winery . . . There I was, a young woman, still a teenager, opening a winery in the rural

South with a bunch of men who were now my colleagues. Not only did they not look like me, but they didn't think like me, nor did we come from similar backgrounds. Everyone looked at me like I had arrived from the planet Mars. I could hear them saying, "She doesn't know what the heck she's doing—she's not going to succeed." They didn't even bother to laugh about me behind my back—they were more than happy to laugh at me to my face.

Despite this, I pushed through because my gut told me to. I would respond, "Well, thank you so much for your time."

I love getting honest and impassioned feedback and criticism, and I try not to be defensive when I get it. When the critiques start, I am probably one of the few people you'll meet who will say, "Yes—please tell me more." I want people to rip apart my ideas sooner rather than later so I have time to fix things before the idea is launched in the broader ecosystem. I would much rather have someone tear up my ideas with passion than let them slide through with indifference. I want my ideas to strike an emotional chord, whether you like them or hate them!

When I became a single mom, instead of retreating into my shell, I found myself saying "yes" to almost everything that came my way because I wanted to stay engaged with the outside world. I also needed to reaffirm my confidence in myself about who Lauren was and what Lauren could get done. It gave me a big boost of confidence during that time to know that I was still respected and wanted as a young businesswoman. I kept my game face on for longer than most people ever do, and I didn't share with people that my marriage and my family had fallen apart. This lasted seven or eight months—I was hopeful that maybe it would all kind of piece back together, and besides, I didn't want anybody's sympathy. I wanted to keep going.

I consider those times to have been the breakthrough moments. It was my choice to take on more than I could realistically handle, but these opportunities kept appearing without my seeking them out. Opportunities kept coming my way, and I continued to accept them.

If I had shared what was going on in my personal life, the people who were sending me these opportunities likely wouldn't have kept engaging me and inviting me to participate because they may have thought, *Oh—she's overwhelmed, she's going through some personal difficulties and getting readjusted. Let's give her some time to get past all this before we put the pressure on.* I purposely didn't share what was going on with my personal life because I didn't want to stop any of the professional opportunities coming my way.

To my surprise, once I was over the sharp, painful hurdle and ready to share what I had been going through, the letters and calls of respect and admiration I received from my colleagues, thanking me for dedicating my time and talent to their businesses and organizations despite my difficulties, were humbling.

When you're in a new or uncomfortable situation, pretend that you have the self-confidence that you might not yet feel. By reaching for those opportunities, you'll prove to yourself that you can do it. There's an incredibly inspiring TED video by Harvard Business School professor Amy Cuddy that discusses the topic of body language and how it shapes who you are.

While the part of her talk about body language was interesting, the presentation really heated up when she started talking about how she was in a terrible car accident when she was nineteen years old, and doctors told her to forget about finishing college—it was no longer in the cards for her. Amy refused to accept this verdict, however, and she worked as hard as she possibly could to graduate. It took her an extra four years, but she did it.

Amy went on to graduate school at Princeton, but she felt terribly out of place among all those super-smart people. The night before she was supposed to give a twenty-minute talk in front of a group of twenty of her peers, Amy was so afraid of being unmasked as "an imposter" that she announced to her faculty advisor that she was quitting. Luckily, her advisor refused to accept her resignation, telling her:

"You are not quitting, because I took a gamble on you, and you're staying. This is what you're going to do. You are going to fake it. You're going to do every talk that you get asked to do. You're going to do it and do it and do it, even if you're terrified and paralyzed and having an out-of-body experience, until you have this moment where you say, 'Oh my gosh, I'm doing it. Like, I have become this. I am actually doing this.'"[6]

By forcing herself to do the things she feared most, she was able to overcome those fears and succeed.

As I was building my own career and success, I took on more than I could handle. I said yes more often than I really should have. I pushed through. I didn't want anybody to feel sorry for me. Nobody wants to spend their day with Debbie Downer. If the cup isn't half full, then add water. Stay the course, stay focused in down times, and never let people know what difficulties you're going through. You don't want people to think that you're overwhelmed or incapable of taking on a new project, a new opportunity, or a new board seat. Doing this in my life has saved me over and over again.

I've never seen a clear-cut path in front of me, but I've always known that I'll figure out exactly what I want to do, and I'll learn what needs to be learned to get the job done. I took on all that I could in my professional life because I was confident that opportunities would allow me to accelerate my professional growth and expand both my horizons and network. I was also confident that taking on all these opportunities would help me reclaim my voice and individuality in both business and personal circles. At the time, the outcome was undefined, but I knew that it would redefine me.

I need to let you in on one more piece of advice. As much as I believe in the importance of planning for your success, you've got to leave the door open for the unexpected—the serendipitous opportunity that you definitely didn't plan for. Sometimes, unexpected opportunities can be the most profitable—not only in terms of money but also in terms of your own long-term success and happiness. Embrace these moments with an open mind and a readiness to adapt because they can lead to growth and achievements beyond your original plans.

FOR REFLECTION

- Always push ahead.

- Surround yourself with an inner circle of true friends who push you to stay the course in difficult times.

- Refine what determines the barometers of your intuition, and once that is solidified, learn to trust your gut.

- Hone a methodology for your personal decision calculus that will carry you through your career and life decisions (see Chapter 11 for more information about "decision calculus").

- When people show you their true colors, believe them. Don't make excuses for other people's negative behaviors. Rise above them and work around or away from them.

- Show that you can persevere with grace during difficult situations. Problems are a part of life, and we all encounter them, but how you handle them will be most memorable.

- Be open to receiving feedback and constructive criticism.

- Try to be self-aware and learn how other people may perceive your words and actions. It will help you adapt how you communicate and become more effective.

11

Don't Be Afraid to Negotiate

(Finessing a Successful Negotiation)

NEGOTIATION ISN'T SOMETHING I'VE ALWAYS done well. It's something I learned through trial and error, and I made many mistakes before I figured out the right way to negotiate. Today, I have unshakable confidence. If you don't genuinely have it for yourself, then trying to play the part will eventually enable you to display and demonstrate the confidence you may not feel deep down inside; see Chapter 10 for the story of Amy, a woman who played the part of "confident woman" so well that she eventually became one.

When I co-founded Sugarleaf Vineyards, I was the stereotypical city girl: A fast-paced, fast-talking individual who expected that everything important happened at lightning speed all the time. However,

I soon learned that not only was I dealing with a male-dominated industry, but also these men were older and more mature and seemed to be in no hurry to make decisions or act on opportunities—or challenges—the moment they presented themselves.

Instead of experiencing the lightning-fast action I had cut my teeth on growing up in the city, I faced a much slower way of doing business. I also discovered that business in the South isn't done the same way it is up North. Culturally, it's night and day. And while this slower-moving culture most certainly does have its charms, it was something I was definitely not used to, and it caught me completely off guard.

When I made the move from my initial role within Gen Y Capital Partners as founding partner to my proposed new role as managing director, I was concerned that my responsibilities might become a bit unbalanced, and not in my favor. I knew if I didn't say something about my concerns, everyone would have expected me to take on the additional responsibilities without the proper compensation. I also knew that taking on the responsibilities of managing director would cost me some entrepreneurial opportunities, so I had to figure out a good way to negotiate so I would ultimately get what I knew I deserved. If you don't learn to speak up for yourself, you may miss out on opportunities or get stuck doing someone else's work.

In the end, I had dinner with Jeremy Johnson, my partner at Gen Y Capital, where I laid out my terms, which were about as frank and straightforward as I could imagine. I made a list of all the activities I had been doing on behalf of the firm, all the roles and responsibilities I had assumed, and the period of time I'd been doing them.

I quantified the data in real numbers and very clearly stated how many additional hours I had put into the job that I wasn't expecting to put in based on my original involvement. I explained what it would have cost the company had we been paying someone else to handle these roles and responsibilities and what kind of equity anyone else in this same role would have received. I put it in easy-to-quantify terms so that there were no ifs, ands, or buts about whether I was right or wrong. The only question was what amount of compensation was appropriate.

MAILLIAN

WHAT I'VE LEARNED ABOUT BUSINESS FROM MY COLLEAGUES

1. **Don't peak in high school.** This is my shorthand for being secure in your own quirks, individual interests, and talents, with little concern for what is popular or conventional. The unconventional is what gets you noticed, hired, and leads toward success.

2. **Pick up the phone or go to lunch [with your colleagues].** In short, don't rely on social media, texting, and email to fully replace relationships—rather, let them be the connective tissue that allows your in-person (or verbal) interactions to be fully effective. Also, sometimes you don't want to have a full conversation about a difficult topic in writing.

3. **Get out there—network, socialize.** Join a book club. Be active in an association. Learn things. You won't get your next opportunity unless you meet the people who can introduce you to it.

—**ERIN FULLER,** *President of Coulter and former President of the Alliance of Women in Media Foundation*

The only way you get autonomy in the corporate world is either to earn it or to go in with it. The same applies to start-ups and a structure that works for you. Either you earn it or you come in with it. In my successful negotiations with Jeremy Johnson (mentioned earlier), I melded the two options!

When I talk about finessing a successful negotiation, I mean learning how to negotiate the best deal you can in the most effective and efficient way possible, using every single tool at your disposal. It's learning how to engage in smart negotiation but also learning how to tailor your communications to your audience and use your personal powers of persuasion and reasoning to get what you want. Whether I'm cutting great deals by way of good valuations or good equity positions in the companies that I'm investing in, negotiating for clients, negotiating terms of a strategic partnership or media buy or sponsorship benefits, or any number of other business transactions, I draw from my very deep treasure chest of techniques and tactics, which are, for the most part, the same negotiation skills that I originally learned and honed at Sugarleaf Vineyards during the course of operations. The fundamentals are the same.

Lauren

MAILLIAN: NEGOTIATING

Do your research. Prepare as if you're pitching for a client, but what you're really selling is you.

I had to change my narrative to get what I wanted, which was my first experience with learning that I needed to be deliberately intentional but not excessively blunt. I quickly learned that "direct" and "aggressive" were not mutually exclusive. And once I figured that out, I soared! Of course, as a naturally direct and forthright person, this wasn't easy for me to do because I'm no-BS and to the point; whether you like it or not, you're going to hear my opinion. But I have to remember to tailor my message to the person I'm talking to and say what I have to say in a respectful way without wasting my time.

There's very little gray area with me. While I do appreciate the importance of learning when and how to finesse your negotiation, I also value those who can get to the point and give me additional insight as necessary, and people value and appreciate that same quality in me. I don't want my time wasted, and I pride myself on not wasting other people's time as well—you'd be amazed at how rare and respected that is. That in itself is a magnetic force for opportunities to flow your way. When and if you can be expected to make something happen in short order while maintaining the highest level of professionalism and integrity, you'll be top of mind for some amazing invitations.

How you treat people is a critical aspect of any negotiation. A little bit of respect goes a long way. Why? Because everyone wants to feel big, like they are important and that they matter to others. This is a critical consideration when you're working with anyone, but particularly when you're working with someone new or whom you've recently met. The person who you think has the lowest standing in an organization may very well exert the greatest control over the calendar of someone you have a meeting with.

The assistant may be the rising star or the person closest to the inside track because they know the granular details better than the boss. Remember: Successful people aren't afraid to hire people who are smarter than they are. You never know who really runs the show! What we were all told as children is certainly true today: "Never judge a book by its cover." I don't let people mistake me for something I am not, and you will never know someone else's true potential if you don't let them know that they matter.

When I had my winery, I needed to work well with members of my team whose families had been farming for generations. This meant communicating effectively with them and making sure they knew that I respected them and that I treated them like the important people that they were. I depended on these men and women to successfully execute the many different tasks involved in making an award-winning wine, so they were extremely important to me.

I stuck out like the sorest of thumbs, the oddest possible ball, the least likely to succeed, but I was determined to be accepted and respected and to make the company a booming success. After joining every organization, committee, and board, as well as taking on major responsibilities that benefited the entire industry and finding an appropriate place for my city-girl marketing and media savvy, respect and acceptance came. Once you gain that trust and respect, the naysayers will quickly become your admirers and supporters.

When you're heading into any kind of negotiation, make sure you know what you're getting yourself into. Do your research. Prepare as if you're pitching for a client, but what you're really selling is you. You should always keep track of any accomplishments at work (see Chapter 8 for more about tracking your accomplishments and the concept of "claim it and shine").

Did you head up a project? Put it down. Did you recruit an amazing employee? Duly note it. Did you woo that unobtainable client? Don't keep it a secret. Try keeping a work journal and logging both daily tasks and big wins. Often, people don't realize the depth of their responsibilities and accomplishments until they see them itemized in an organized way. This is something only you can do for yourself—no one knows your work better than you do.

If you think that you're going to be in a difficult situation, make a list of pros and cons, or make a list of your points and why you support them. Be able to solidify your opinion. Be able to back up what it is you're asking for. Be able to quantify your request.

Take the time to do your homework so that when you're ready to communicate, whether it be by phone, email, text, or whatever, you are as prepared as you possibly can be. Know your deal breakers. Create a timeline for what you want. Know what you want and need, and what you would like to have. But remember: always keep your strategies to yourself.

Being armed with information is meaningful; knowing when to use it is powerful. Examine your leverage—how to create it, strategize and work with it, and when best to use it. Set the tone for your negotiation to make your motivations and intentions clear. It's also good to take the time to understand who you're negotiating with.

Ask yourself the following questions:

- What makes them tick?
- What do you think they will want out of the deal?
- What motivates them?
- What's urgent versus important for them?
- What are their deal breakers? What are your deal breakers?

Not only will you be better prepared, but you will also show that you're a smart negotiator and that you've considered more than one outcome.

Don't apologize. It lessens the weight of your argument, which goes back to being firm in your decisions. Avoid saying "I feel," "I need," or similar phrases. Keep everything focused on facts, numbers, and information. Your boss isn't responsible for paying off your credit card debt or funding your summer vacation.

When you're negotiating with your boss, base your arguments strictly on what you've done for the company. Be firm and deliberate when discussing your accomplishments. Stay away from mushy and unassertive words like "kind of," "sort of," "maybe," and the like.

If you're closing a deal, don't linger or talk out of nervous energy. State the terms, seek confirmation, and discuss the next steps. Don't give the other side the chance to change their minds or spend time waffling on inconsequential details. Be clear, be firm, be progressive, be gracious, but know when to go for the big points versus spending time on the smaller points. You have to know when to hold out for what's most important to you.

Always remove yourself from an adverse or uncomfortable situation with dignity, grace, and elegance. How you leave a bad situation speaks volumes about your character and integrity, and you never know when your paths may cross again. Always wear velvet gloves. Don't let the person you treat poorly today be the person you desperately need tomorrow.

Lauren
MAILLIAN

WHAT I'VE LEARNED ABOUT BUSINESS FROM MY COLLEAGUES

According to David Jones, former Global Chief Executive Officer of Havas, the world has always been obsessed with youth, but this young generation is unique for several reasons:

4. **Technology**: They are more knowledgeable than any previous generation, thanks to the power of technology.

5. **Social Responsibility**: They are more socially responsible, seeing the big issues facing the planet and wanting to do something about them.

6. **Power and Influence**: They are the most powerful generation of young people we've ever seen, understanding the power of digital and social media and how to harness it to drive and effect change.

This generation also possesses a built-in sense of what the new world of business needs to look like and is actively creating and molding their businesses around this model. They see the high unemployment rates around the world and understand the need for growth, but they also recognize that growth must happen in the right way—without compromising the planet and its people. This generation is proving that making money and doing good are not mutually exclusive.

It's also important to keep in mind that sometimes you have to crouch to conquer. For instance, when you're just starting out in your career, you may have to work at a discounted rate or be willing to take on roles and responsibilities that are outside of your given title in order to build some experience. Further on in your career, you may have to play by rules that you don't think are fair, or you may be faced again with the possibility of having to take on a role or responsibility that you think is outside of your job description or level of expertise in order to get what you want.

The decision calculus looks different for everyone, but you need to consider (1) how big the prize is, (2) how much you feel you can or cannot see the light at the end of the tunnel, and (3) how important it is to you to really achieve what you want. If you feel doing any of this will truly leverage your career or give you unprecedented access, then do it, but make sure you don't lose sight of your own values.

The negotiations you set have to be true to you and what you believe in. Many people have asked me to work with them or advise them for nothing—it happens all the time. I respect people who aren't afraid to ask for something they want and are transparent about their lack of resources, but at some point, you also have to reflect and ask, "What helps me further my personal mission?" If it isn't going to help you further your personal mission, then it doesn't make sense for you to get sucked into a vacuum of additional responsibility for which you have no major upside.

FOR REFLECTION

- Be confident. If you're not naturally confident, then try faking it until you make it!

- It's valuable to occasionally take on additional responsibility in an informal way to get your feet wet, so long as you keep track of the responsibilities that have gone above and beyond the initial scope of your work.

- You can't always put compensation first, especially when you're a rookie. Work hard, create a track record through experience, quantify your contributions, and know what you want to earn based on market standards. Ask for it when your contributions are concrete and valuable instead of premature and hypothetical.

- Know your audience and how to adapt your narrative for maximum effectiveness.

- Show that you value everyone's time, including your own. Explain the big points first and give granular detail when it's necessary.

- Treat everyone like a rock star.

- Know when to hold out for what's most important to you.

- Never apologize in a negotiation.

- Learn how to control the intensity and direction of your communication, whether it's through your words or your actions.

- Always leave a negotiation gracefully.

$$\left(12\right)$$

Rebound Gracefully

(Keep Calm and Carry On)

PEOPLE ARE JUDGED BY THE way they handle stressful situations. Attacking adversity head-on, rebounding gracefully, and finding a new route or a new approach toward reaching my goals has served me well. It hasn't been easy, but the results speak loudly. I believe that I learned to rebound gracefully when I was forced, at age thirteen, to deal with my parents' breakup in addition to the pressures of being a teenager.

I was an independent city girl going through adolescence, and all I wanted to do was hang out with my friends. But everything at home was falling apart, and the environment was incredibly stressful. It was up to me to find my own calm. This is when I first learned the importance of stepping outside of whatever crazy situation I'm in to gain perspective, because when you're in it, sometimes you can't see past it.

The lessons I learned from this painful experience many years ago came in handy when the founder of a company I advise asked for advice about a senior management issue. I gave the same advice that had been given to me, which was to step outside the situation to gain perspective. She immediately did just that and was able to refocus her energy on the success and growth of her company instead of petty disagreements (read more about this below).

Keep your head held high and realize that there's power in being graceful and calmly standing your ground. In the end, if someone else speaks badly about you, does something they know they shouldn't be doing, or says something they know isn't true, it will reflect badly on that individual, not on you.

People aren't stupid—they can see when someone is trying to tear down someone else. People who act with impulsive, irrational, or disrespectful behavior will inevitably lose the respect of others. So if you sit back and refuse to participate in actions that you know are beneath you and you rise above them, then it's you who will come out on top. I believe in karma—that those who have acted with honor and integrity in this world will be rewarded for their actions, and that those who have wronged others will one day have to answer for their actions.

I think people often feel like they are gladiators when they end up in adverse situations. But sometimes you have to step outside the situation, hold your head high, take a deep breath, keep your mouth shut, and say to yourself, "I'm going to let this person do that. I'm going to let this person run him or herself into the ground and dig his or her own hole." Maintain your own grace, dignity, and pride when someone is trying to sabotage you, because it not only sends a powerful message of truth to the world but also others will soon recognize the sabotage for the bad behavior it is.

Whether in an office back-and-forth, a tit-for-tat via email, or on the telephone, it takes a bigger person to say, "I will no longer participate in this." Half of the time, people who are out to hurt you want to know they can get under your skin, but you send them a powerful message when you let them know they don't have that control over you. When you learn to step outside the situation and look at what's really going on, you will not only bring down the level of intensity, but also you can strategize about how to get what you want from the situation and how to work with and around the situation until you can make it go away. It's extremely difficult to pull yourself out of the muck when you're emotionally and mentally caught up in it. You must step outside of it to see the clear path forward.

WHAT I'VE LEARNED ABOUT BUSINESS FROM MY COLLEAGUES

I am fortunate that Matthew Harrington at Edelman introduced me to Gail Becker, the Chair of its Canada, Latin America, and U.S. Western Region. He saw something in me that reminded him of Gail, which is flattering in and of itself. Gail is proof that you can persevere and succeed in just about anything you put your mind to. Politics, journalism, public affairs, media, and public relations—there is nothing she hasn't done and can't do well. I admire her even more for using her success as a platform for other women by serving as the Chair of Edelman's Global Women's Executive

Network (GWEN), the company's effort to increase the number of women at the senior-most levels of the firm. Here is Gail's advice for success in business:

1. Take risks.

2. Spread your wings and make yourself uncomfortable. Nothing great was ever achieved through being comfortable and staying still.

3. My willingness to try anything once, no matter how uncomfortable it has made me, has had the greatest impact on my success.

4. Self-challenge has always been my greatest motivation. Thinking I can't do something dares and forces me to try it. I remind myself not to be afraid of failure.

I once told a colleague that no one really cares about who said what to whom and when. The only thing people will care about is who wins in the end—whose company works better, looks better, and makes more money. When I said those words to her, it was like a cloud had been lifted from her eyes.

She said, "You're right. I need to go work on my company because that is exactly what the other person doesn't want. They want me to take my eye off the ball and divert my energy into battling them instead of building and running my company." She immediately focused her energy back into operating her company instead of managing a catfight. And she has done very well, moving past the pain and growing her business.

I believe that the graceful rebound speaks very much to owning your own voice and being in control of where you're going. And even though sometimes it may not look like you're in control of where you're going, in this day and age, with blogs and all sorts of online outlets, you have the power to (mostly) control what your digital footprint looks like and also the ability to directly affect what your colleagues think of you, such as by keeping people informed about your events and accomplishments. You're able to command so much more on your own terms than any previous generation has been able to do.

Lauren

MAILLIAN: REBOUNDING GRACEFULLY

> Step outside the situation to gain perspective. You can't see past it or through it when you're in it.

Sometimes I have to focus all of my energy on staying the course. When I was going through my divorce, I would tell myself that the reason it was so dark was because I was still in the middle of the tunnel. I had to remind myself that I had to stay calm even though I couldn't yet see the light at the end of the tunnel. But I knew that it was there and that I would eventually feel a flood of warm sunlight.

Remember that it's always in your best interest to stay calm and carry on. Truth be told, no one really cares about the elephant in the room once people stop buzzing about it. What they do care about is if you're still in the game after the dust settles and how you let the pieces fall.

I now realize that there's an art to slowing down the game a little bit, especially when somebody wants to antagonize or create an inflammatory situation. It's like a tennis player who takes control of the pace of a game by hitting baseline strokes that slow down the pace of a match. Know the importance of being silent, acting without haste, and speaking with an informed opinion. It commands more respect from others.

I used to be very impulsive: I rushed to do everything. I rushed to say everything. I rushed to get emails out. But I've learned that I don't have to always be the first to respond, nor do I have to have the first word. It takes great restraint to say, "Not so fast—I'm going to slow this down and you're not going to have this control over me. I'm going to control the pace and direction of this exchange."

I've realized that I'm best served when I think about what it is I want to say and when I am thoughtful and deliberate in my communication. But once I utter those words or commit them to writing, I'm 110 percent unwavering and confident in my position. I used to instantly respond to every text message I received without fully considering my options. Part of it was probably immaturity on my part because I was young, or maybe it was my excitement.

It's easy to get excited and jump up when you feel like you've been wronged or in any way disadvantaged. But I've found that you're so much more respected and appreciated and admired by others when you (1) take the high road and (2) are deliberate in your communication.

This is not to say that being timely isn't important—being timely is important, but not acting with haste is even more important and really commands the respect of everyone else around you, which ultimately gains you credibility.

It's okay to wait to return a call. It's okay to hold onto the email or text response for a while. Sometimes I'll wait twenty-four or even forty-eight hours to reply to an email that I think is heavily charged with items that need to be carefully handled. It's important to take your time to absorb information and communicate not only effectively but strategically, and to make sure that your voice is deliberate.

Text messages and emails are ubiquitous because we use our phones, iPads, and computers so often, whether at home or at work. You've probably felt like you had to get that message off of your screen as quickly as possible by responding to it. It takes a lot of self-control and deliberative thinking to sit back and say, "Now I'm going to really be thoughtful about this response and not shoot something back off so I can get it out of my inbox."

As long as you at least do that and carry on and prove yourself, you're creating a new track record that can catapult you into whatever it is that you do want to do. Maybe you won't always achieve each and every goal that you set for yourself, but you may start up an entirely new company that has the potential to become super successful, or you may get that promotion that you've been angling for. It's probably not realistic for anyone to assume or even hope that everything they touch will turn to gold. I get that. But you'll never know unless you try—at least once!

Stay calm, carry on, embrace those opportunities that align with your personal goals as they present themselves, and before you know it, you've created a new track record of success for yourself in whatever your chosen profession might be. Before you know it, you're six or twelve months down the road and chipping away at those ten thousand hours that Malcolm Gladwell says it takes to build the expertise to get to the top in your chosen field.

FOR REFLECTION

- It's not the problem that people care about, but rather how you dealt with the problem and the issues along the way that matters most.

- Mentally, step outside a challenging situation, gain perspective, and figure out a way to emerge stronger than before.

- Always be the bigger person and rise above the nonsense. Remember: The actions of those who would tear you down are a reflection of them. Don't let someone win by dragging you into their mud puddle.

- Own your voice, control your narrative, and be deliberate in your communication.

- Learn when to be prompt and proactive in your communication, but also when you're best served by taking a day or two to collect your thoughts and analyze the situation before acting. Not every response needs to be a knee-jerk one.

- Stay calm.

Live Life on Your Terms

(Decide What Success Means to You)

YOUR REPUTATION BELONGS TO YOU. Allow no one else to define you. I hold myself to high expectations, and I've always been this way. I strive to improve myself more than anyone else ever will. This has been true for everything I've done in business—from the winery to Luxury Market Branding (LMB) to Gen Y Capital Partners—and everything I will do in business.

I think everyone knew what I was capable of doing with LMB, but what surprised many people was how quickly I had LMB up and running. I knew that if I was going to make a go of this business, I had to have it up and running and producing great work as quickly as possible. The longer I waited, the less buzz there would be around the business, and the greater the chance prospective clients would go elsewhere.

So I set my bar very high, and LMB was in business. In truth, clients could have gone to a company that had been established for years, with a longer track record of success, but they knew what to expect in terms of the quality of my work and work ethic, so they came to me.

I set the bar pretty high at Gen Y Capital when I stepped up to the plate and agreed to be the firm's managing director (see Chapter 14). In reality, I had been acting as managing director for the seven months prior to formally taking on the role.

Everyone looked at me and said, "Lauren, you've been doing all the responsibilities of managing director. You've been making capital calls, writing investor quarterly update memos, deal sourcing, working with the team on due diligence, conducting venture partner calls, leading investment committee meetings, structuring the fund, closing subsequent rounds of investors into the fund, being the point person for the legal formalizations of our investments, and doing the accounting."

MAILLIAN

WHAT I'VE LEARNED ABOUT BUSINESS FROM MY COLLEAGUES

Caroline Ghosn, Founder, CEO, and Artist, exudes strength and epitomizes tenacity. She's one of the few young entrepreneurs I admire for her unshakable confidence. Caroline is equally receptive and perceptive, and she serves as a clear example of what fearlessness and determination can achieve. Regardless of the expectations she holds for herself, she's already attained success on her own terms. Here are some characteristics that Caroline finds important for success in business:

1. **Find Your Passion and Focus on It.** You spend more time building your career than any other aspect of your life (statistically speaking). Make it count, and make it something you're proud to leave behind.

2. **Tenacity Has the Greatest Impact on Success.** No matter what comes my way, I won't quit. And I won't.

Caroline's approach to business is a testament to the power of persistence and dedication. Her ability to maintain focus on her passion, coupled with her unwavering tenacity, has been instrumental in her success. She serves as a role model for entrepreneurs who aspire to build meaningful and lasting careers.

It was true: I had been overseeing everything and performing the duties of managing director, going far above and beyond the responsibilities of a founding partner, even without being specifically asked to do so. But with my name associated with the firm, I instinctively assumed these responsibilities.

I redefined what success meant to me once again when LMB helped a high-profile owner of a major beauty brand get her new business up and running. The company had previously been in a licensing deal for several years, which allowed its brand equity and likeness to be used on products it had no control over.

Consequently, the quality suffered, and the brand languished. After living out its non-compete clause, the owner started a brand-new company with an entirely new name and came to me for help in building this new brand. We explored what the new brand would look like, its narrative, ethos, and mission, who the customers would be, and how we would reach them. Ultimately, it was a great success, with the new brand gaining a presence in stores nationwide as well as online.

Just as you need to decide for yourself what success means to you in business, the same applies to your personal life. You can let others define success for you, but in my experience, that's a sure way to live a life full of lost opportunities and regret. Remember: You are the one who will someday look back at your life and legacy and decide if it was good—and lived with as few regrets as possible.

I really appreciate how Arianna Huffington defines success. She says, "We need a third metric, based on our well-being, our health, our ability to unplug and recharge and renew ourselves, and to find joy in both our job and the rest of our life. Ultimately, success is not about money or position, but about living the life you want, not just the life you settle for."[7]

Surround yourself with people who keep it real, keep you grounded, and are willing to point out your flaws. One of the most effective ways to do this is by creating a personal advisory circle, a group of individuals who are different from those you might seek for career guidance. We all have room for improvement, but we're generally more receptive to constructive criticism from a select few we respect and admire.

Striking the balance between being confident and comfortable in your own skin—so much so that you exude leadership and command respect—while staying humble enough to embrace opportunities, recognize setbacks, and proactively learn from them, is incredibly delicate. I strive not to be defensive when receiving criticism or feedback. Instead, I focus on being introspective because, at heart, I am very self-aware. For those who are naturally competitive, it's essential to avoid thinking that there's nothing to be gained from the opinions of others. Be introspective, process the feedback, and learn from it.

Regardless of my stance on an issue, I always try to understand how my words or actions might have negatively influenced someone else's perception. This practice not only makes me a more effective communicator but also serves as a gentle reminder of when and how to adapt my speech and behavior to ensure I'm understood in any given situation.

Staying grounded and connected to the moral compass that defines you is something you cannot outsource. This spiritual support is what drives you to excel and be whole and completely fulfilled. One powerful way to maintain this connection is through corporate social responsibility (CSR). CSR has become increasingly significant in the business world, with companies large and small—from McDonald's, Walmart, and Levi Strauss & Co. to Gap Inc. and many start-ups—seeking to be positive forces in their communities and the world at large.

To achieve this, they champion values such as human rights, environmental management, fair employee treatment, and nonprofit partnerships. They promote philanthropy, employee volunteerism, and community investment, aligning their business practices with a greater purpose.

THE IMPORTANCE OF PSR (PERSONAL SOCIAL RESPONSIBILITY)

One of the key goals of an entrepreneur is to give back to the community in ways that will help effectuate change and innovation at the grassroots level. I recently participated in the Girls Who Code Summer Immersion Program, which partners with AT&T and Intel, to name a few. The organization exposes high school girls to coding and teaches them about technology through a hands-on program.

I believe that we'll see more women entering technology fields and the start-up community once they feel equally informed, educated, and empowered to do so. One of the most rewarding things about the event for me was hearing what the girls had to say about the experience after the fact. What a humbling feeling to know that I was able to inspire these budding entrepreneurs:

> "I was struck by Lauren Maillian's focus on the future and her long-term goals; she really emphasized how important it is to have an ultimate goal in mind and measure every opportunity in terms of how it will help advance you toward that goal."

> "I will remember the fearless attitude of [Lauren], her drive, and her advice."

But while companies are embracing CSR, individuals can do much the same by defining, embracing, and promoting their PSR. I think everyone wants to do work that makes a difference in people's lives, and it is certainly the case for me and for most of the entrepreneurs I know. Yes, at the end of the day, we want to make money, but that isn't all that drives us. What drives us is knowing that we're building something bigger than we are that will have a positive impact on our investors, employees, vendors, customers, communities, and other stakeholders.

What's Your PSR?

- What would you change for the better?
- What problem do you want to fix most?
- What are your non-negotiables?
- What are the things that define you?
- What are the roles and responsibilities that you're willing or not willing to do?
- What will help you get there?

My PSR is that I want to create a new way of being successful, which is both personally and professionally fulfilling and allows me to live the life I desire. I want to change the definition of success to include the personification of success as well as the paths one must take to become successful. I also want to redefine what a typical successful person looks like—no longer just Ivy-League-educated corporate men.

I want to create and do something that has real meaning and purpose for people while also being financially successful—not only for myself but also for those who will fill the jobs I want to create. I'm grateful that I've been able to employ people and see others thrive— it's not all about me.

My dream is to do something that enables me to give back on a corporate level, not just through monetary donations. I've always done a lot of giving back through my businesses. At LMB, we do some work for philanthropic organizations pro bono, and at the winery, we had several cause-focused partnerships with a percentage of tasting-room profits going to charity.

I would love to be able to do something far larger, something where 5 percent of my company's annual revenues are devoted to nonprofits that are making a difference. This level of giving could potentially impact the lives of hundreds or thousands of people and make the world a better place. As an entrepreneur, this would be a dream come true.

Lauren

MAILLIAN: GIVING BACK

Life is about more than me. Life is about more than you. Simply put, make a difference.

You have to be very self-aware and then use this self-awareness as a compass when you make decisions. So, ask yourself these questions:

- How well do you know yourself?
- Why do you make decisions?
- What's important to you?
- What makes you happy?

If you don't know the answer to these questions, and others like them, you will find yourself either spending an exorbitant amount of time analyzing your options before you make a decision or that the decisions you make are wildly inconsistent. Neither outcome is good for you or your company. Remember that life is a journey to figure out what is most important to you. We live to have experiences that help us refine what we want and how we want to live—it's a continuous, lifelong purpose.

If you don't feel self-aware, then you should take some time to evaluate yourself and gain an understanding of what your decision calculus looks like for making decisions that you will consistently be comfortable with. My own decision calculus for saying either "yes" or "no" to each opportunity that I encounter, big or small, is the same regardless of what industry it's in.

I go through the same motions and ask myself the same exact questions every time a new opportunity arises. Will I always be proud of this decision? Will it further my professional pursuits and enhance my experience? Will I be able to maintain happiness in my personal life given what is required of me professionally?

We all need a process for making decisions that enables us to have a decision calculus that best aligns with what we want for our lives. When this decision calculus is clearly reflective of your values, needs, and desires, then you can trust your gut that the decisions you make both personally and professionally will be the right ones for you.

This is the way I feel about life in general, not only about career:

▶ Always be yourself because everyone else is taken.

▶ Be hungry to succeed, not thirsty for attention. It's more important to be well-connected than it is to be visible.

▶ Try to emulate those people who inspire you, but don't assume that the popular people are successful. Some of the most accomplished professionals keep low profiles for very good reason.

▶ Sometimes, especially when you're going for growth and exciting opportunities, say "Yes!" And then, when you look back, you'll find that you're amazed by what you have accomplished.

I have decided to live life on my own terms, and that's exactly what I do. I'm independent, and I make decisions that are in the best interest of me, my family, my companies, and my clients. I highly recommend that you do the same—live life on your terms. Decide what you want from your life and what your minimum requirements are. Then seek out situations and opportunities that mesh accordingly. Even if you don't find the degree of success that you seek, you'll be far more satisfied with your life if you follow your own path rather than one someone else has laid out for you. Remember: Each of us only has one shot at life. Make the most of every day and have no regrets.

FOR REFLECTION

- You are your reputation, not your company or your title. It's all about you—the impressions you leave, the interests you pique, the conversations you start.

- Surround yourself with people who keep it real, are grounded, and who you can trust to tell you the honest truths that others often hide. Create your personal advisory board and challenge them to point out your flaws, along with feedback about what you could be doing better.

- Don't be defensive when receiving criticism. Receive it. Process it. Learn from it.

- Stay grounded and never lose sight of your moral compass.

- Evaluate and define what impact you want to have on the world and on the lives of others.

- Create your PSR and ensure it includes your non-negotiables and states what it is that defines you.

- Live life on your terms. Do what works best for your life as defined by you and no one else.

Embrace Failure

(But Learn from Your Mistakes)

Y OU DON'T HAVE TO ACTUALLY fail to embrace failure. You can feel the fear of potential failure and then either choose to succumb to it or face it and move forward. This was the case shortly after we started Gen Y Capital; we were looking for a managing director to run the fund. Our strategy at Gen Y is to invest in early-stage companies that will benefit from the leverage provided by many of the world's top young entrepreneurs.

We were all successful young entrepreneurs who joined forces because we were hyperconnected to brilliant and innovative entrepreneurs who were building businesses (we heard about them from our inner circles and had early access to top-tier deals) and because we could add strategic value.

We always intended to hire a managing director for Gen Y Capital—someone with extensive investment expertise who would oversee the day-to-day operations of the fund. We had lots of meetings with potential investors—sometimes I'd go by myself, and sometimes with my partner, Jeremy Johnson—to talk with people who we thought would be interested in investing in Gen Y Capital, either as a way of syndicating their own approach to investing in early-stage companies or because we provided access to the kinds of deals they wanted.

In many of those meetings, prospective investors would look at me and ask, somewhat incredulously, "You want me to give you a couple million dollars and trust that you're going to hire a rock-star managing director to run the fund? Why would I give you money based on your great thesis but not be able to see and meet and get to know the person who is actually going to oversee this strategy day to day?"

Lauren Maillian

WHAT I'VE LEARNED ABOUT BUSINESS FROM MY COLLEAGUES

When it feels bad in your gut, it is bad. Don't let that little voice in the back of your head tell you otherwise; it most likely is bad. Somehow our guts just know before our minds can figure it out. People will let you down. They will lie. They will cheat. They will kick you when you are down. But it is in those moments that you find your true inner strength, develop your character, and test your integrity. Know the path in front of you will never be easy, but do not give up. When you think you can't go on, go to sleep and wake up the next morning ready to tackle whatever is thrown at you. Whatever it is, it's never as bad the next morning.

At the end of the day, success should only be determined by you—not by external factors like the media, your friends, competitors, or even your family. When everything is said and done, you are accountable to yourself and who you want to be.

I've been very quick to get over the woe-is-me situations—the "Ugh, why is this happening to me?" and "I don't deserve this!" moments. Although it certainly feels like the world is against me at times, and yet going so well for others that I think it shouldn't (don't pretend you don't have those moments and days, too!), being able to move past feeling sorry for myself or blaming my failures on others has allowed me to learn quickly and create new opportunities. Dwelling in the past doesn't allow you to move forward, learn, and get back on the path to success.

—Amanda Pouchot, *Brand Director, MET-Rx & Body Fortress*

Of course, they had a point—why should they?

It got to the point where people would look at me and say, "Why aren't you doing it—why aren't you the managing director, Lauren?"

I never planned to be the managing director of Gen Y Capital Partners. Truth be told, I didn't think I was qualified for the job—at least not in a formal sense—and I was afraid of failing at it. I didn't have the years under my belt managing investment funds on Wall Street, nor had I been investing in tech start-ups in Silicon Alley—or

Valley. We were interviewing people who had fifteen years or more of experience working at some of the top growth and early-stage venture firms in New York City and elsewhere.

But what we learned from these interviews was a surprise to us. While these candidates had the deep, formal, calculated investment knowledge that the position required, they didn't have the entrepreneurial minds that we were looking for. And that was a problem because having an entrepreneurial mind is what resonated best with the founders of the early-stage companies we wanted to invest in.

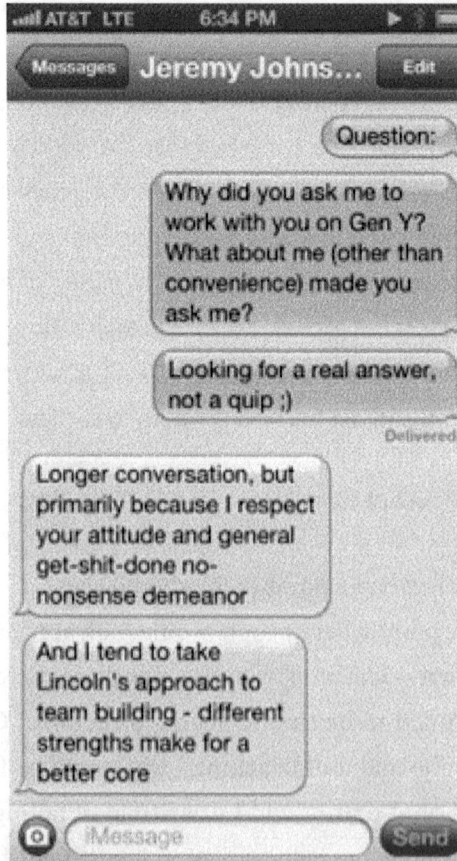

Message with venture fund partner, Jeremy Johnson

So I didn't have the experience on Wall Street managing funds, but everyone—my partners, existing investors, and potential investors—knew how hard I worked and how I gave everything I had to whatever I chose to do. And they wanted me to take on the job of managing director.

Managing a venture fund requires many of the same skills that all really good entrepreneurs have. It requires good intuition and judgment of character, and an ability to deeply analyze business operations, structure, and revenue models. It requires wide connections that are deep enough to be able to open doors for companies to help them accelerate their growth. People looked at me and said, "You have all those things."

I was excited and a little unnerved by the challenge, but I agreed that I should be the managing director of my fund. It wasn't easy, and the potential for failure was there, but I made it work. I hunkered down and cut out anything that wasn't absolutely necessary from my schedule, including unrelated social encounters. I focused on what I knew was going to create great value for Gen Y Capital Partners. I still stayed relevant, however, by networking and letting people know what I was up to—accepting certain opportunities and invitations to events to meet more people and see what synergies existed—but I couldn't possibly explore outside interests as much while I built up Gen Y Capital Partners.

Lauren

MAILLIAN: EMBRACING FAILURE

As long as you learn from whatever failure it is that you've experienced, you really haven't failed at all.

When people heard about me starting Gen Y Capital and then running it, I received more and more invitations to speak and attend conferences, events, and roundtable discussions. I accepted as many of these invitations as I could because it gave me the chance to introduce early-stage companies and potential investors to Gen Y Capital.

As a result, I slept very little during the first two months. There wasn't enough time to go through the arduous process of valuing the business I was in the process of selling, while at the same time devoting attention to my clients on the Luxury Market Branding side, let alone eat and spend time with my children.

I had been charged with the task of devising the investment thesis and objective for Gen Y Capital Partners, overseeing operations and the formation of this new investment entity, and learning whatever it was that I didn't already, but desperately needed to, know at the time.

Failure was constantly at the front of my mind, but I pushed through and somehow got it all done. The rush of building something new kept me up at night, and the adrenaline and excitement kept me moving forward. I told myself, "You're going to get this all done. You're going to make it happen." My mind raced even when my body wanted to sleep.

There are at least a million-and-one sayings and famous quotations about dealing with failure, and I'm not going to repeat them all here. But I will say that as long as you learn from whatever failure it is that you experienced, you really haven't failed at all. I know people say this all the time, but I truly do believe it.

Today, I am so crystal clear about what I want for my children, what I want for myself, what I want out of my professional and personal lives, what kind of people I want to work with, and the kind of man I want to be with. At this point in my life, I have a breadth of business experience that I probably could not have had any other way. And I have learned a lot of hard lessons along the way.

So, what does failure look like to you?

➤ When you didn't close the deal you should have?

➤ When you didn't make the money you should have?

➤ When your reputation is tarnished among the businesspeople with whom you want to work, or in public?

To me, nothing is really a failure unless it adversely affects your reputation indefinitely. And even if your reputation is tarnished, in my opinion, unless you've done something super unethical or illegal, there's always a way to turn it around.

Heck, look at the long line of celebrities, musicians, politicians, businesspeople, and others in the public eye who have staged dramatic comebacks from the worst circumstances possible, from Bill Clinton to Martha Stewart to Tiger Woods. Here in New York, Anthony Weiner and Eliot Spitzer. At a point these people were blacklisted from their elitist circles, but now they are once again on invite lists around town.

The point is, as long as you have a plan and stay consistent and forthright, time heals many trespasses, and if these high-profile folks can rebuild their reputations, then so can you!

In business, I've learned that many people are afraid to be transparent. That is, they're afraid to lay all their cards on the table. I have found that transparency is a real asset in business, and I make a point of working this way all the time. I'm certain that because I'm transparent, I command people's respect.

My integrity is ingrained in every aspect of who I am. The easiest, best, and most effective way to build rapport and strong connections with others is to become so transparent that people are genuinely surprised by your candor. I have found that people really want to work with a person who is real.

I'm also a big believer in fessing up to the fear you feel instead of trying to pretend it's not there. Fearlessness is not the absence of fear; it's the acknowledgment of fear and then moving forward despite it.

I agree with a June 2013 post by Seth Godin on his blog that touches on this concept. In short, Seth said that when you ignore fear or try to will it away, it gets stronger. The only way to defeat fear is to acknowledge its existence and move forward anyway. It's amazing what you can accomplish when you tolerate fear instead of denying it.

You shouldn't limit yourself because of fear. You never know what you're capable of doing unless you try. I was nervous about taking on the job of managing director at Gen Y because I didn't have the formal background, but I had experience on my side. I jumped in with both feet and made it happen. I take risks when I'm convinced I can add value and know that the experience will be worth it—even if I fail. It can be a little scary at times, but I know I'll always learn valuable lessons from both my successes and failures. Instead of asking, "What would I do if I wasn't afraid?" I think the right question to ask is: "Is it worth doing even if I fail?"

FOR REFLECTION

- Every time you're faced with a major decision, ask yourself: "Is it worth it even if I fail?" If the answer is "yes," go for it!

- Try not to constantly recalibrate your definition of success— you'll never know when you've achieved your goal if you keep changing the target.

- Trust your intuition when it aligns with your moral compass and personal mission.

- Be transparent.

- Seek to work with people of integrity. You can always find higher ground when you're working with good people.

(15)

Make It Look Easy

(Don't Look Like What You've Been Through)

I THRIVE UNDER PRESSURE. MY NATURAL tendency is to take on far more roles, responsibilities, and opportunities than I probably should. This has been true for as long as I can remember. But by doing this, I gained a lot of confidence in my abilities at a very early age. I started looking, sounding, and acting more confident—and this opened new doors for me. The more doors I walked through, the more doors opened. It was a domino effect—once it started, it didn't stop.

When I started the winery, I was transitioning out of my full-time modeling career and becoming a full-time student, working toward my undergraduate degree in International Trade and Marketing at the Fashion Institute of Technology. I had made some money through modeling and wanted to invest it in real estate.

Initially, I purchased the land as an agricultural tax deduction, but I decided to turn the property into what would eventually become a thriving top-tier vineyard, which I then leveraged into a boutique wine brand. I took every opportunity while I was in school to create case studies and business plans for the winery tasting room I knew I would eventually build on this property. I used my time at school to work toward my end goal of starting the winery, although, if I'm being honest, I still harbored a desire to create a business in the fashion industry.

MAILLIAN

WHAT I'VE LEARNED ABOUT BUSINESS FROM MY COLLEAGUES

Rachel Noerdlinger, Global Communications Expert and Partner at Actum, is like me. She thrives under pressure and values being open and honest. This approach has led to her many accomplishments and allowed her to find success on her own terms. She has always pushed ahead in the face of adversity and has reminded me to do the same.

I first met Rachel when she was with The Terrie Williams Agency; her client was the preeminent Black women's magazine *Essence*, where my mother, Audrey Adams, was the director of corporate public relations. Rachel used to chuckle when she watched me, an eleven-year-old girl, leading my babysitter around the Essence Music Festival in New Orleans, commanding attention and making moves.

Flash forward, and Rachel has become a fixture in my life, beginning when I interned for her at The Terrie Williams Agency. I continue to learn a lot from her:

1. To succeed in business, you must nurture and groom relationships. Networking is essential to brand-building. Follow-up is a golden rule.

2. Stay connected and embrace new communication methods and trends.

3. Study your trade. Know the news and be adaptable.

4. If someone tells you "no," create your own niche.

5. Surround yourself with people who lift you up.

MAILLIAN: MAKING IT LOOK EASY

You've got to take time in your schedule to recharge your batteries and build up your reserve of passion and energy.

When I was in the last semester of my senior year of college, I was pregnant with my first child and taking twenty-four credits (three credits over the max for the semester, with special permission from the dean of the college, of course).

I was in my last trimester and I wanted to finish up as quickly as possible so I wouldn't have to return to college with a newborn at home, which also coincided with the public opening of the winery's tasting room in August 2007. My son was born in December 2007, and I took my final exam the morning I went into labor. My son attended my graduation in May 2008 when he was six months old! I thrived under the pressure of everyone expecting me to cave.

Was it easy? No—definitely not. Did I make it look easy? Yes, I think I probably did. As someone important to me once said, "You don't look like what you've been through." I think I could and maybe should adopt this as my own personal motto.

Work with passion and energy. But you can't always be passionate and energetic 24/7. You've got to take time in your schedule to recharge your batteries and build up your reserve of passion and energy. It's easy to fall into the trap of working far too many hours and not taking meaningful breaks.

The Hidden Brain Drain Task Force at the Center for Work-Life Policy is concerned about this very topic. According to the Task Force, "62 percent of high-earning individuals work more than 50 hours a week, 35 percent work more than 60 hours a week, and 10 percent work more than 80 hours a week." And this doesn't include the commute back and forth to the office from home, which can easily add another hour or two to each workday.

Lauren
MAILLIAN

WHAT I'VE LEARNED ABOUT
BUSINESS FROM MY COLLEAGUES

1. I think too many people behave like the hare, not the tortoise, from the old fable. This doesn't mean we can't make an impact early on in our lives and careers, or chalk up plenty of successes along the way. But I've realized that wisdom is gained through experience, some victories can be short-lived, and true impact comes from lasting results.

2. There is also great value in listening, absorbing, and reflecting before taking action. I sit in too many meetings and discussions where people are simply taking turns waiting to hear themselves talk and not actually engaging. This is a recipe for wheel-spinning, self-referential inaction in the end. And it's not very nice.

3. Life is not a zero-sum game. Others don't have to lose for you to win. Give others credit, help them succeed, be kind and open-hearted. Sound trite? Then why don't more of us do it? Better outcomes happen because of better behavior.

—Jaime Prieto, *Advertising Agency CEO*

Vacations also take a beating among high-performing professionals, with 42 percent taking ten or fewer vacation days a year and 55 percent reporting that they have had to regularly (and voluntarily) cancel vacation plans. I have also been guilty of doing this, but it's something that I hope to diminish if not eradicate entirely as I advance in my career.

The harder you work—no matter what kind of work it is you do—the more important it is that you take regular breaks from the day-to-day grind. Whether it's yoga, meditation, working out, reading books, getting extra sleep, or spending more time with your friends and family—whatever it is that enables you to recharge your passion and energy—figure out what that looks like for you and then make it a consistent part of your life. Make sure that you always bring the best version of yourself to the table.

FOR REFLECTION

- Make it look easy even though it's not.

- Work hard, with passion and energy.

- Take care of your mental and physical health during down-times to gear up for more mental exertion when times get hectic.

- Take contemplative time for yourself to evaluate where you're going.

- Learn to unplug so you can be the best version of yourself when it's time to resume the fast-and-furious work regime.

- Keep your personal difficulties private if there's a chance they will curtail opportunities of interest.

- Find the relaxation regimen that works best to help you recover and then make it a regular part of your life.

(16)

Optimize for Satisfaction

(Maximize Opportunities for Happiness)

I PUT MORE STOCK IN MYSELF than anyone else can, and I know I'm a better support and inspiration to others when I'm the very best version of myself. Period. On that, I do not compromise. By being the very best version of myself and making sure that others have the opportunity to experience this version of me in every facet of my life—from work to personal—my opportunities for happiness are multiplied many times over. Like a powerful magnet, I attract people who are like me (hardworking, smart, successful) and also dedicated to making big plans in their lives and executing and carrying them out.

I was at a dinner with a group of entrepreneurs hosted by Joe Lonsdale, who started Formation 8, a venture firm located in the San Francisco Bay Area, and is a previous founder of Palantir Technologies and Addepar. He was also instrumental in building Clarium Capital with Peter Thiel.

In his early thirties and wildly successful, Joe was here in New York when he invited me to the dinner. When I arrived, it turned out that I was the only woman at the table. It was eleven guys and me. I laughed and said, "I don't know if I should feel special or feel set up!" Of course, they were all super nice, and they turned out to be a group of the most incredible start-up founders possible.

Carter Cleveland, the founder of Artsy, was there, along with the founder of Warby Parker eyewear, Dave Gilboa, seated to my left, together with other rock stars in the start-up community from companies like Square and Uber.

Most of these guys were in their twenties—like me—and no one was more than thirty-five years old. I knew four of the people at the dinner, and the rest I'd never met.

There I was, sitting at the table, and everyone who didn't know me asked, "How do you know Joe?" Of course, I was asking myself the very same question about each one of them. Asking and answering this question provided us with a great way to break the ice as we introduced ourselves, talked about our entrepreneurial journeys, and got to know one another.

Not only did we get to tell some interesting stories about how we met Joe (and some were quite comical), but we inevitably found out that we had other interests, people, companies, and investments in common. By the time we finished our meal, I liked them all, and they liked me. I expect I'll keep in touch with many of the entrepreneurs I had dinner with that night. We have many mutual connections and interests that may cause us to connect again and again else-where, through other organizations, people, business opportunities, and events.

So how did I meet Joe? I met him through a colleague named Jake Kloberdanz, who I met through other colleagues who connected us as the rare young entrepreneurs who were crazy enough to go into the wine business. Jake co-founded a company called OneHope Wine; the sale of a bottle of each of his varietals of wine supports a different philanthropic health cause.

I've rarely encountered a young entrepreneur who knows anything about wine, so we immediately hit it off and began exploring opportunities for me to invest in some of his projects. We had only been working together for a short time, but we established a friendship. He got to know me as a person, and since he had already seen my work ethic during all of our due diligence research, he decided I should meet Joe Lonsdale, the chairman of his board. See how it always goes back to creating networks and the importance of having people respect you for the work you do and the value you can add?

Joe ended up coming to New York, and we set up a time to have coffee, and from that point forward we've been friends. We don't have any direct work relationship or investments we're working on together, but I know he recognizes that being surrounded by smart, driven, hardworking people makes his future possibilities endless. It's a relationship I value—he's super down to earth, and he's one of the smartest people I've ever met and definitely the most accomplished young person I know personally.

In recent years, a lot of research has been done (and no small number of books have been published) on the topic of happiness. According to *Delivering Happiness at Work*, a workplace consultancy started by Tony Hsieh, CEO of Zappos.com, "happy employees are committed, drive sales, and are about 43 percent more productive." Unfortunately, in typical organizations, "72 percent of the workforce is unhappy," and there is a cost of approximately "$13,000 a year in lost productivity" for each unhappy employee.

Other people notice rarefied work ethic and dedication and want someone who's passionate and committed on their teams, and dedication creates opportunity. Most boards are by invitation, not application. You want to be invited into the circles, boards, councils, and committees where all the leaders are—the sandboxes of successful people. You've got to demonstrate to others that you're passionate, committed, and will give 110 percent to everything you do.

Mellody Hobson, who we first met in Chapter 5, was presented with the opportunity to work on Bill Bradley's political campaign in 2000. She didn't want to leave her company, Ariel Investments, but the opportunity to work on Bradley's campaign was too good to pass up. She told Bill words to the effect, "I will work for you part-time in the evenings, but I will give you full-time effort, and you will never feel like I work for you part-time."

And so, for almost two years, she went to work at Ariel from 6 a.m. to 3 p.m., and then she switched gears and worked for Bill Bradley from 4 p.m. to 10 p.m. The people she worked with saw her work ethic firsthand, and ultimately, many of those people offered her the opportunity to serve on a number of high-power corporate boards.

MAILLIAN: OPTIMIZE FOR SATISFACTION

Always be the very best version of yourself, and make sure that others have the opportunity to experience this version, too, because your opportunities for happiness will be multiplied many times over.

You can end up in the big leagues right away when you give the right person reason to believe in you and in the quality and caliber of your work ethic. You never know who you're going to meet. You never know who's watching.

There's something to be said about being hardworking while other people are taking notice. I worked really hard for nearly twenty years, and now I'm part of a powerful ecosystem of like-minded people who dream big and do big like me. We inspire one another, we support one another, we vouch for one another's credibility, and we often end up pursuing opportunities together and working together.

The most amazing thing you can do when you become influential is to be in a position to actually effectuate change. Company and nonprofit boards are a great place to do this. Existing members invite other people they like, respect, trust, and network with to work with them on these boards. And when you become established on a board, you'll be able to do the same. Share what you know—it's the quickest and easiest way to attract amazing opportunities.

Don't sabotage your chances of success or ruin your credibility ever. Being impressive is mostly about being reasonable in your projections and hitting them consistently. So that's what you need to do and communicate to the outside world. I am motivated by the big, overarching, lofty goal. But what motivates you may be something different.

Don't miss opportunities where you can grow quickly—go where there's growth. This looks different for each person. You should be willing to move sideways and down to take on new experiences. And that's exactly what I've done in my own career. When I started the fund, I was actually thinking about going to grad school to get my MBA.

I was at a place in my life where I was thinking, "Okay, everyone thinks I've been super successful for my age, and I guess I have if

I really think about it. I also already have my children, and they're happy and healthy and thriving. So, what's next?"

I decided that I was going to sit for the GMAT and apply to a top business school—University of Pennsylvania, Harvard, or Stanford— and I was going to pack up my family and make the move to my top choice. I was convinced that I needed an MBA to take the next step in my career and to push my path to success on an even higher trajectory.

Lauren Maillian

WHAT I'VE LEARNED ABOUT BUSINESS FROM MY COLLEAGUES

I admire Jeremy Johnson, Co-Founder and Chief Executive Officer of Andela, for admitting his weaknesses and trusting me to carry his weight on our team. At one point, it felt like I was being given all of the work when, in fact, I was being given all of the responsibility. Absent those responsibilities, I would not have created my own track record of success in the start-up and venture communities. I respect him immensely for believing in me and pushing me to do more than I had originally bargained for. Moreover, he taught me the art of knowing my audience and how to be a good team player in a partnership.

So, while I was making big plans to sit for the GMAT and enroll in a top MBA program, Ed Mathias of the Carlyle Group said to me, "Lauren, you don't need an MBA—absolutely not. Everything you learn when you get an MBA you've already learned. Half of the reason for getting your MBA is building a network, and you've already got a network. The other half of it you're going to learn in real-life experience in less time than it would take you to go to school and get an MBA."

And then I had the opportunity to start the fund, and my MBA plans immediately ended up on the back burner. Looking back, I can see that Ed was right. I learned more from starting Gen Y Capital Partners. I learned even more about legal processes, strategy, business formation, finance, venture evaluations, technology, and start-ups than I would have ever learned in two years of business school plus a year of preparing and applying to get in.

Go where there are opportunities that allow you to grow quickly and enhance your experience. And have a personal mantra. Tell yourself that you're going to succeed. Look at yourself in the mirror and repeat your mantra to yourself—own it. If there's something that you want for yourself, set your mind on it, and be comfortable embracing it and owning it. Remember: You don't need permission to be ambitious, but you need to give yourself permission to be ambitious.

Even though I am incredibly optimistic, I generally look at the worst-case scenario as my indication of whether or not an opportunity is going to be worthwhile. It's not by any means an indication of my real-life expectations, but it sets the framework for my tolerance.

Go for exciting, amazing opportunities where there's potential for growth, whether it's the financial kind of growth, with a really exciting salary and performance-based bonuses; a growth of experience; a personal growth of testing yourself and your capabilities; a growth of exploring who you are and what you're passionate about; something new and exciting to add to your resume, or a personal challenge—you take it on in that moment.

You don't necessarily always have the luxury of thinking about how it is going to look to everybody else. Sometimes, when the opportunity and potential for personal growth is so large and exciting, you grab the opportunity to advance.

I think the luxury today is that, especially with social media and all these real-time channels, we get to own the narratives of our lives. We get to be responsible in large part for the stories we tell about ourselves. We can't be responsible for how other people perceive us, but we can certainly be responsible for what we share and how we share and communicate our decisions to the world. It's up to us to take the reins and to set our course and go.

FOR REFLECTION

- Invest more in yourself than anyone else can.

- Don't allow people to pigeonhole you.

- Quickly and kindly validate yourself and reject stereotypes.

- Try not to make assumptions about others. There's nothing worse than a hypocrite.

- Learn that sometimes flattery comes packaged in a barrage of inappropriate questions with a hint of disbelief. In these cases, learn to nod, smile, and say thank you. It'll catch them off guard and level the playing field.

- Determine what satisfaction and a fulfilled life look like for you. Prioritize your satisfactions and make attaining them a large part of your life.

- Be passionate, committed, and show dedication.

- Rest easy knowing that it's okay to have a full plate and overwhelming responsibilities if it advances your satisfaction quota.

- Figure out a way to make worthwhile opportunities work even if the time in your schedule seems nonexistent. You can't turn back time to get back an offer or opportunity, and there's little worse than feelings of regret about not doing something you were curious about and really wanted to do.

- Don't miss opportunities where you can grow quickly.

17

The Path Forward

(Planning for Your Worst-Case Scenario)

ONE OF THE BIGGEST MISTAKES people make in business and life is assuming that the ground beneath them will always be stable.

Well, it won't.

Life will throw the unexpected at you. Markets will shift. Laws will change. Investors will pull out. Customers will move on. And if you aren't prepared for your worst-case scenario, you aren't really prepared at all.

You need to be thinking ten steps ahead, always.

For years, I built my businesses on the foundation of hard work, strategic thinking, and results. I never relied on labels or certifications. I refused to apply for the minority-owned business certifications that many others sought because I wanted my success to stand on its own.

And it did.

I built brands, secured partnerships, raised capital, and scaled businesses, all without ever using those certifications as leverage. It felt good. It felt like proof that my work was undeniable, that I didn't need anything extra to get in the room.

Then the pandemic hit.

Suddenly, there were funding opportunities, grants, and relief programs exclusively for minority-owned businesses. There was a brief window to self-report and be eligible for government contracts and initiatives to support companies like mine.

But I had spent years rejecting anything that could be perceived as a handout. I wanted my success to stand on its own—undeniable, unshakable.

And yet, at the same time, something unexpected happened. Every opportunity I had worked for, every door I had knocked on, suddenly flung open. Brand partnerships, investment deals, board seats, global speaking engagements, everything cascaded into my lap at once. It felt like life's acceleration, a moment I had unknowingly been preparing for.

But I also knew one thing for sure: this window wouldn't stay open forever. So I prepared to seize the moment at all costs. leveraging every opportunity, making every move count, ensuring that when the tide shifted again, I wouldn't just be standing, I'd be ten steps ahead.

But still, I hesitated.

I wondered if I had been wrong all those years. Had I left money on the table? Had I made things harder on myself than they needed to be?

I recall my father always telling me that my baseline was 2x everyone else's standard—because it had to be. Because I wasn't expected in those spaces and rooms. Working twice as hard has always been my norm. It's half of how I've been able to live The Path Redefined—not just once, but over and over again.

One win has never been enough for me. I know the winning window is finite, fickle, and often unfair. So I never wait for it to stay open—I move, I build, I set my own standard. Because at the end of the day, real power lies in defining success on your own terms.

How many can say that their expectations of self exceed the expectations of others?

Fast forward to today, and many of those same diversity-driven initiatives are being dismantled. Funding is disappearing. DEI programs are being cut. The same doors that were briefly open for founders like me are now being shut again.

And here's the lesson: the game is always changing.

You can't build your success on assumptions. You can't assume that what works today will work tomorrow. And you definitely can't assume that the opportunities available to you now will always be there.

So, what do you do?

Do you ride the wave, or do you set the rhythm of a current that keeps pulling you to greatness?

Do you let the world determine who and what you can be, or do you create a strategic plan for your vision, one that accounts for every possible outcome to ensure your greatness?

The diversification makes all the difference. Diversification of your skills, your network, your experiences, your travels, and your investments. Because in life, something will always fail to deliver on a promise, on an expectation, even on a dream. But there is no defeat when something else has come to fruition in its place.

And while there are no guarantees, there are guardrails, good vibes, and great choices that we can make every day, when our plan to live The Path Redefined is clear.

So you must prepare for every possible outcome.

IF YOUR ENTIRE BUSINESS RELIES ON ONE CLIENT, ONE CONTRACT, OR ONE MARKET—YOU'RE VULNERABLE.

IF YOU HAVEN'T DIVERSIFIED YOUR REVENUE STREAMS, YOUR SKILLS, OR YOUR NETWORK—YOU'RE AT RISK.

IF YOU'RE BUILDING BASED ON HOW THINGS ARE INSTEAD OF HOW THEY COULD BE—YOU'RE ALREADY BEHIND.

Survival in business isn't about how smart or talented you are. It's about how adaptable you are. The ones who stay ahead aren't the ones who get lucky. They're the ones who see the shifts coming before everyone else and make their moves accordingly.

Success isn't just about what you build—it's about how well you can protect it.

And I am a big believer of Execution Over Visualization

A lot of people talk about success as if it's a mystical thing that only a chosen few can achieve.

They say... Just visualize it. Manifest it. Speak it into existence.

And hey I do believe in vision. I believe in setting clear goals, in knowing exactly what you want, in seeing yourself already achieving it.

But I also believe in action.

You cannot think your way into success. You have to move.

"Faith without works is dead," says the holy book.

And I must admit this doesn't come easily because I used to struggle with structure. I was a night owl, staying up late and pushing through projects at odd hours. It worked for a while, but eventually, I realized I was fighting against myself.

So I made a shift.

I committed to discipline.

Now, my mornings are intentional. They start with movement—hydrating, checking in with myself, stretching, strength training. Before the world even wakes up, I've already taken control of my day.

That's not luck. That's not motivation. That's execution.

Because execution will take you places that motivation never will.

So put simply, you don't need another strategy session, you need to start.

You don't need another business book, you need to make your first sale.

You don't need to wait for "the right time", you need to move with what you have, now.

Don't be stuck in the planning phase, convincing yourself you need one more piece of information before you start.

Your dreams don't work unless you do. Period.

THE PATH REDEFINED IS A MOVING TARGET

Yes, indeed it is.

And that's why with success you may never feel like you've arrived.

I wrote the first edition of *The Path Redefined* a decade ago, and I can tell you, I am still redefining my own path every single day.

I have accomplished things I never thought possible. I've built businesses, sat in boardrooms, raised capital, launched initiatives, and stood in spaces I once only dreamed of.

And yet, every time I reach a new level, there's another level waiting.

Just as I was navigating one of those moments, standing between what was and what could be, I found myself in a full-circle, serendipitous encounter that reminded me exactly why I believe in divine timing and preparation.

This is what The Path Redefined looks like in real time. You prepare, you build, you stay ready, and then life presents you with an opportunity that demands the full weight of who you've become.

And just like that, you step into it.

So you see, there is no final destination. There is no finish line where you suddenly feel like you've made it.

The moment you stop growing is the moment you start losing.

The moment when you realize that becoming is more about shedding and chasing as you transition into new phases.

And the funny thing about new phases is that everyone talks about embracing them, but no one talks about what it actually takes to scale these transitions and step into newer versions of yourself, without guilt, without feeling stuck.

We romanticize growth. We admire the idea of transformation. But do we really talk about the cost?

Do we avoid the conversation about how stepping into new versions of ourselves can be messy and uncertain?

How it may even feel like losing, especially when it's necessary?

How often than not, it's terrifying?

And when we are terrified, fear disguises itself as practicality:

"I am still far behind."

"No way I'll ever achieve this because, well... I'm 20, 30, or 40, or 50."

"What if this doesn't work out?"

"Maybe I should wait until I feel ready."

That's fear pretending to be logic.

Fear convinces us that holding on is safer than stepping into what's next. It tells us that maintaining the familiar is better than facing the unknown. And so, we stay.

We stay in jobs we've outgrown.

We stay in relationships that no longer align.

We stay in mindsets that no longer serve us.

Not because we want to, but because we fear what happens when we finally let go.

And I get it.

But after years of building and becoming, my answer to this is simple: **fear thrives in the absence of action.**

And I'll tell you why...

You cannot build something new without first creating space for it.

If you've ever had to truly let go of something—a role, a title, a relationship, a version of yourself—you know it doesn't feel like freedom at first.

It feels like a loss.

Even when you know it's the right thing.

Even when you've outgrown it.

Even when you're stepping into something better.

There's still grief in what you leave behind.

And that's what stops most people.

We think, "If this was the right decision, why does it feel so hard?"

And we forget that difficulty is not a sign you made the wrong choice but proof that change is happening.

You cannot build something new without first creating space for it.

So, what does it really take to step into a new phase? Not just in theory, but in practice even when it's uncomfortable?

- ▶ **Make peace with uncertainty.** You will never have all the answers before you take the leap. No one does. Clarity doesn't come before action—it comes from action.

- ▶ **Redefine failure.** Most of us don't fear change—we fear making the wrong choice. But failure isn't an ending. It's just new data. You adjust, you pivot, you move forward.

- ▶ **Detach from old identities.** If you've built success in a certain role, industry, or way of working, it's tempting to cling to it. But who you've been is not the limit of who you can become.

- ▶ **Trust yourself.** Not in a vague, motivational way—but in a practical way. You have already overcome things you once thought would break you. That alone is proof that you can handle what's next.

I hope you have clarity on the moment you're in, especially if you're standing at the edge of something new.

And if you're in that place—standing between what was and what will be—know this:

THE ONLY WAY FORWARD IS THROUGH.

And on the other side of fear?

That's where you become who you were always meant to be.

That's also why I created The Confidence Compass. Because even after everything I've done, I know that confidence isn't a one-time achievement—it's something you have to actively build, over and over again.

Some people take over the world once and assume they'll never have to break a sweat again.

That's a mistake.

Every new challenge requires new effort. Every new level demands a new version of you.

Success is never one and done. It's a continuous evolution. And that's because the confidence that got you here may not be enough to get you there , the skills that built your first success may not sustain your next one, the work never stops, and neither should you.

This is what The Path Redefined is all about.

It's about understanding that success isn't a fixed destination but an ongoing commitment. It's about knowing that no matter how far you've come, there is always more growth ahead.

So the question isn't "Have I made it?"

The question is, "Am I willing to keep going?"

Because that's the real path to success—and it's yours to define.

Acknowledgments

LOVING, HEARTFELT THANKS TO MY children, Jayden and Chloe, for inspiring me to be my best, and for giving a true purpose for my success.

Lifelong thanks to my parents, Audrey and Brian, for giving me all that they could, but also never letting me live my life in a bubble of unrealistic expectations, despite my surroundings. It has certainly kept me grounded, hungry, and determined. And for that I thank you both from the bottom of my heart.

An immense amount of gratitude is owed to my mother for instilling values in me at a young age, and for giving me exposure to opportunities that cannot be duplicated and that have uniquely molded who I am and what I believe in. Thank you for helping to make everything I have accomplished possible by stepping in to co-parent as a grandmother so that I could realize new potential and make the necessary commitments of myself and my time.

I also owe thanks to my father for demanding so much of me so early on, which has forced me to be disciplined in my work ethic and taught me to work well independently and to be self- motivated. And to my grandma Bunny, my grandfather Floyd, and my grandma Ruby for raising my parents with a solid foundation from which to raise me, and for instilling fear in me as a child of the consequences that would result from not doing my best—Lord knows, I was scared beyond belief to ever disappoint any of you!

I would like to thank each one of my wonderful and generous business colleagues, friends, and family members who helped bring this book to life. Specifically, I am forever grateful to Gail Becker, Lisa Nicole Bell, Selena Cuffe, Chloe Drew, Kathryn Finney, Stacy Francis, Erin Fuller, Caroline Ghosn, Adam Hanover, J. Kelly Hoey, Carola Jain, Jeremy Johnson, David Jones, Ido Leffler, Matt Mullenweg, Rachel Noerdlinger, Morin Oluwole, Amanda Pouchot, Jaime Prieto, Kathleen Warner, and Donna Williams.

A special thanks to Mellody Hobson for taking time between Starbucks board meetings to chat with me about her perspectives on success and what separates her from the rest of the pack.

And last but not least, a deep thanks to all those who didn't believe in me or in my abilities. Your lack of belief only made me stronger and drove me to persevere despite your lack of support. This has reinforced why I seek motivation only from within myself, and it reminds me that you have to work for what you want, and want it more for yourself than anyone else ever will.

About the Author

LAUREN MAILLIAN IS A TRANSFORMATIONAL business strategist, investor, and brand-builder known for driving growth, unlocking new revenue opportunities, and scaling consumer brands, media platforms, and technology companies. She has spent her career at the intersection of marketing, investment, and business development, helping companies redefine their industries and accelerate expansion.

At just nineteen, Lauren co-founded an internationally recognized, award-winning wine brand, making her the youngest self-made winery owner in the U.S. Since then, she has played a pivotal role in shaping billion-dollar brands, advising Fortune 500 companies, and repositioning global businesses for sustained success.

Lauren is also a seasoned investor, launching Gen Y Capital Partners, an early-stage investment firm, and amassing a personal investment portfolio now exceeding $4 billion. She has been instrumental in the public and private markets, including advising on the $913 million public listing of e.GO Mobile (NASDAQ: EGOX) and supporting the strategic growth of brands like Amazon, JPMorgan Chase, Amex, Estée Lauder, and P&G.

Beyond business, Lauren is deeply committed to fostering innovation, diversity, and leadership. She serves as Jury President for the Cartier Women's Initiative, advises Overtime Select (a women's sports league backed by Jeff Bezos and Drake), and sits on multiple advisory boards, shaping the future of business, brand positioning, and strategic investment.

A sought-after speaker and thought leader, Lauren has spoken at The Wall Street Journal's Women In Series, Fast Company Innovation Festival, American Express Business Class Live, and World Expo Dubai. She has been featured in *Forbes, TechCrunch, The Wall Street Journal*, CNN, *Vogue Business, Fast Company, Cosmopolitan*, and *Ad Age*, and co-starred on CNBC's *The Unstoppables* and Oxygen's *Quit Your Day Job*.

Named *LinkedIn's 50 Inspirational Black Women in Marketing* and *The Root 100 Most Influential African Americans in Business*, Lauren continues to shape the conversation on entrepreneurship, investment, and brand transformation.

She holds a B.S., *magna cum laude*, in International Trade and Marketing from the Fashion Institute of Technology. Lauren currently resides in Puerto Rico with her family.

ENDNOTES

1   Baer, Drake. "How Arianna Huffington Networks Without Networking." Fast Company. September 25, 2013. http://www. fastcompany.com (accessed November 21, 2013).

2   Smith, Chris. "Don't Hire Entrepreneurs; Hire Entrepreneurial Spirit." Harvard Business Review. February 1, 2013. http://blogs.hbr.org (accessed November 21, 2013).

3   Maillian, Lauren. "The Serial Entrepreneur's Guide to Reinvention." Fast Company. January 27, 2012. http://www.fastcompany.com (accessed November 25, 2013).

4   Weymouth, Katharine. "How do you 'lean in' if you don't have someone to lean on?" Washington Post. March 22, 2013. http://www. washingtonpost.com (accessed December 30, 2013).

5   Kasanoff, Bruce. "Three Words That Will Transform Your Career." LinkedIn. May 30, 2013. http://www.linkedin.com (accessed November 30, 2013).

6   Cuddy, Amy. "Amy Cuddy: Your Body Language Shapes Who You Are." TED Talks. October 2012. http://www.ted.com (accessed December 1, 2013).

7   Huffington, Arianna. "Huffington on Sandberg: To Lean In, First Lean Back." The Wall Street Journal. March 11, 2013. http://blogs.wsj.com (accessed December 5, 2013).

www.ingramcontent.com/pod-product-compliance
Lightning Source LLC
Chambersburg PA
CBHW071206210326
41597CB00016B/1691